REALITY
FUNDRAISING

Author of Five Best Selling
Fundraising Books

Bob Hartsook

With Introduction by Robert G. Swanson

Additional copies of this book are available from the publisher. Discounts may apply to large-quantity orders.

Address all inquiries to:
ASR Philanthropic Publishing
P.O. Box 782648
Wichita, Kansas 67278
Telephone: 316.634.2100
Facsimile: 316.630.9993
e-mail: info@ASRpublishing.com
web site: www.ASRpublishing.com

Other books on philanthropy by Bob Hartsook include:
Closing that Gift!
How to Get Million Dollar Gifts and Have Donors Thank You!
Getting your Ducks in a Row!
Nobody Wants to Give Money Away!
On the Money!

Edited by Denise Rhoades
Cover design by Lori Cox
Photograph of Bob Hartsook by Mark McDonald

Printed in the United States of America by Mennonite Press, Inc.

Library of Congress Control Number: 2005924105

ISBN# 0-9663673-7-5

"These best practices are sometimes brilliant, sometimes simple, but all are employed and delivered by professionals with a passionfor their organization and a dedication to their profession."

REALITY FUNDRAISING:

▶ Proven, Practical Ideas for the Enlightened Fundraiser

Author of 5 Best Selling Fundraising Books!

Bob Hartsook

With Introduction by Robert G. Swanson

ASR PHILANTHROPIC PUBLISHING

TABLE OF CONTENTS

DEDICATION

This book would not have been possible without the hundreds of practitioners who took time to express their best professional practices. To each of them this book is dedicated.

In addition, my son, Austin has always shared the dedication page.

Introduction

Robert G. Swanson
President, Hartsook Companies

Identifying and harnessing the knowledge and experiences of others has always been a Bob Hartsook strength. In his 30-year nonprofit career, Bob has steadfastly embraced the expertise and success of professional fundraisers for insights that one seldom finds in the latest all-encompassing Fundraising Professional's Encyclopedia.

Reality Fundraising, Bob Hartsook's sixth book, continues his commitment to help fundraisers understand the basics of their craft while at the same time grasping the "street-wise" nature of successful fundraising. In *Reality*, he gives the four basic steps of fundraising – Identification, Cultivation, Solicitation and Appreciation – a real-world face as dozens of fundraisers from more than 30 states share their successful tools and strategies with Bob, Hartsook Companies, and now you.

As you read this book you will discover familiar strategies and hopefully find some new ones. These best practices are sometimes brilliant and sometimes quite simple, but they are all employed and delivered by fundraising professionals who have a passion for their organizations and a dedication to their profession. You will find that the fundamental steps of fundraising are best achieved when the successful practices outlined in this book are adopted and employed by you and your organization.

Successful fundraising, as I tell my own clients, is never achieved solely by following the text of a book or locking into a detailed development plan. Fundraisers and their volunteers must be willing to adapt and modify their activities, plans and tools whenever they face hurdles and obstacles. "We can't get a meeting" or their answer is "No" are never adequate replies for the professional fundraiser. If these responses have become acceptable – as a single response from an individual prospect or as the echo of a group of responses over time – your fundraising operation is on a downhill slide. It is heading in the wrong direction.

Bob's book provides more than 100 jewels addressing the issues of identification, cultivation, solicitation and appreciation in a real-life format. Each nugget carries with it the attitude and philosophy that obstacles and hurdles must be faced and cleared. Whether you must go over, under or around them, barricades should be successfully conquered the majority of the time. It is with that attitude and zest that Bob has written and compiled *Reality Fundraising*.

It has been my privilege to work with Bob Hartsook when he served as a lead consultant on one of my own campaigns. It has also been my pleasure to work with him as one of his lead consultants and as the president of Hartsook Companies. In every fundraising endeavor, creativity and perseverance are his distinctive trademarks.

Reality Fundraising is a continuation of Bob's life-long belief that all fundraising professionals and nonprofit organizations can become successful if they will commit themselves to their missions and employ the smartest strategies and the best practices of fundraising. As you will soon experience for yourself, Bob's zeal for his profession is contagious. If you are ready to face *Reality* and raise major gifts for your organization, this book was written with you in mind.

How to Use This Book

As you know, I try to make the work we do in philanthropy simple and stimulating. This book is no different. You do not need to read this book from cover to cover.

As with many of my books I suggest that you review the Table of Contents for a subject of interest to you and turn to that chapter to read the conclusions from the practices and then the actual practices. We have noted everyone whose practice we used in the book and where they are from. I am sure they would not mind a phone call from you or a note if you want further explanation.

In the Index the best practices are listed by organization, as well the author of the best practice.

Enjoy this book and know that from it you can advance the work of your institution.

Bob Hartsook

Note: Those contributing best practices were working with the noted organizations at the time the best practice was submitted.

BEST PRACTICES FOR EFFECTIVE CULTIVATION

Use the 'Five-I Process' to cultivate donors: Identify the prospect. Gather Information. Determine Interests. Encourage Involvement. Secure Investment. Do these in order; don't make the mistake of jumping from the first 'I' to the last.

Duane L. Dyer, ThM
Hartsook Companies, Inc. (San Francisco, Calif.)

*Ideas are like rabbits. You get a couple and learn
how to handle them, and pretty soon you have a dozen.*

John Steinbeck
U. S. novelist (1902-1968)

CULTIVATION VITAL FOR INDIVIDUAL DONORS

For all the talk of foundations and corporate giving, individual donors are still the biggest givers to nonprofits. While it is important to cultivate foundations and corporations through relationship building, it is vital that you cultivate and strengthen the bond between your nonprofit and its individual donors if you really want to raise major money for your organization.

A general rule is that the longer a donor gives to an organization, the greater the loyalty and potential for larger gifts in the future. This is only true, however, if a nonprofit takes seriously its responsibility for ongoing donor cultivation.

CULTIVATION, A YEAR-ROUND JOB

In the Midwest, you get accustomed to seeing wheat fields in various stages of development. If the fields are greener than the greens of St. Andrews, it is winter. If the combines are rolling, it is summer. Whether planting or harvesting, tilling or burning the stubble, the work is never finished. So it is for development and, specifically, cultivation. Cultivation is a year-round activity.

If it is true that your most loyal donors are often your longest-standing donors, and if your most loyal donors represent your greatest opportunities for big gifts (especially planned

1

gifts), then you want to ensure that your organization never takes these donors for granted.

Build a big front door for prospective donor pools, but make sure you spend just as much time guarding the back door. If a major donor drops off the radar screen, find out why. Donor retention is one reason why regular cultivation is so essential. Donor relationships are always easier to maintain than they are to repair. Consider time well-spent in cultivating relationships as time saved in rebuilding damaged relationships.

CULTIVATION IS EVERYONE'S BUSINESS

Have you ever phoned a law firm or visited a doctor's office and been underwhelmed by the service you received from the staff? Somehow you know that the behavior of office staff is a reflection of the whole practice. If a company has a fundamental value of "treating clients with the utmost respect at all times," then that becomes the office culture and the norm.

The same is true for nonprofits. The best cultivation happens when the whole organization (not just the development office or the director of development) has a core value of treating donors well. Make sure everyone in the organization understands the importance of treating donors with deference. "It's how we answer our calls, answer donor questions, answer for our mistakes ..." Donor cultivation is not a one-person or one-department job; it is a necessary mindset that should permeate the entire organization.

KEEP CULTIVATION PROFESSIONAL

As polished, sophisticated and engaging as a fundraiser might be, he should never forget that cultivation is about a professional relationship. It is not about creating a personal circle of friends, but about building friendships for the organization.

Fundraisers serve as ambassadors for the nonprofit. Therefore, a level of dignity and decorum is always in order. Never ingratiate yourself into the donor's world. Never cross that subtle line between personable and personal. Let the donor set the tone and tempo of the cultivation process. Become an expert in body language and voice inflection. Watch for clues and listen for hints to the best methods of cultivation for the ultimate goal of soliciting major gifts.

GOOD CULTIVATION MAKES FOR GREAT SOLICITATIONS

Keep in mind that the goal of cultivation is always to raise major money for your organization. The best avenue for receiving large contributions is through valued donor relationships. Raise your standards for cultivation and you will raise greater gifts – in size and significance – for your nonprofit.

One practice that goes a long way is treating people with respect. Regardless of whether you are networking with community leaders, recognizing the work of volunteers and board members, or visiting with someone who utilizes your organization's services, everyone appreciates being treated with respect. Be careful not to put a mental box around who you believe comprises your donor base. And always remember, networking and building relationships is an ongoing process.

Charlene Lund
South Dakota CASA Association (Pierre, S.D.)

CHAPTER 1
MISSION-MINDED CULTIVATION

MAKING THE MOST OF YOUR MISSION

MISSION (`mishun) [n] *a task that has been assigned to a person or group*

What is the specific "task" for your nonprofit? Why does your organization exist? What would happen if it ceased to provide services? What negative consequences to people's lives (or to the environment, the arts or education) might one expect as an outcome?

The greatest way to attract and identify committed donors is first to have a clear and demonstrative conviction about your organization's value in the world. No amount of hard work and fast-talking can outweigh a concise, yet compelling demonstration of the good your organization achieves in the lives of others.

When it comes to raising major gifts, start with the mission. Make sure you understand and believe your nonprofit to be worthy of support. Then use that confidence to leverage interest among prospective donors who are likely to feel the same way.

As you look for prospective donor pools, consider the people who are directly or indirectly affected and influenced by your organization. Some connections are obvious – universities and their alumni or museums and their regular attendees. But what about less conventional connections?

Ask your staff and board members, "Who has been touched by our organization?" Now look out just beyond these individuals to other creative possibilities. Many nonprofits dismiss their own clients as potential pools for donor prospects. This kind of limited view can cause an organization to miss out on some potentially strong relationships. Ask yourself what connections these people might have and how they could provide an open door for fundraising.

An adoption agency should consider those who have been a part of the adoption process: friends, grandparents, church communities, doctors, attorneys. Ask the people you help if there were individuals particularly touched by the agency's service to them – people who might want to "make this joy possible for other families."

One organization serving low-income, working families with food and medical services realized that many of the single mothers worked for the same company. The organization had always received a modest, obligatory gift from this company. Before the next ask, the staff developed a more personal proposal that shared some of the stories of employees who had been helped by the nonprofit. That year the company increased its giving substantially.

Prospecting for new donors is a limitless ocean of opportunity. Do not miss affiliated donors because your clients are unable to give big financial gifts. They probably are able to offer something else – heartfelt referrals.

IN SEARCH OF THE UNDISCOVERED DONOR

If your organization's mission is meaningful, then there will always be people who feel strongly about what you do as a nonprofit. It is imperative to begin with this conviction: "There are people out there who would be pleased and grateful to be part of this great organization. We just need to find them." Every "no" on the way to locating these "undiscovered donors" brings you closer to your goal – connecting a great organization with donors who care about the mission and who have the ability to give major gifts in support of that mission.

There are many methods for identifying and gathering information on prospective donor pools (child-related, environmental and research/cure-related causes, and arts, education, social services, etc.) – everything from no-tech client, staff, board and donor surveys to high-tech search engines and software. But never let the many strategies available overshadow the mission.

Use creative tools and administrative methods to create a larger donor pool, but take the heart of the mission with you as you do. Keep coming back to the basics. "This is who we are. This is what we do. Where can we find people as passionate about this mission as we are? Now let's go find them and raise money!"

MISSION-MINDED DONORS EQUAL DEEPER COMMITMENT LEVELS

The more enthusiastic donors are about the mission, the more cooperative and supportive they will be in other areas – advancing new programs, new staff, capital and endowment goals. The more connection donors experience with the inner workings of the organization, the easier it will be to generate support – financial and otherwise – for projects and objectives.

By identifying donors who are already earnest believers in your cause and then familiarizing them with the organization – personalizing the relationship – you are not only attracting a new pool of donors, you are attracting donors who come equipped with commitment to the cause.

The mantra of fundraising is, "Everyone is a prospect." This is true, but it is particularly beneficial to clarify your mission and identify prospective donors who are already passionate about your sector of concern (arts, education, children, homelessness, etc.).

MISSION-MINDED MARKETING

It is surprising how many hard-working organizations remain virtual strangers in their own communities even after years of service. They work so diligently and their mission is so important that they can easily assume that "everyone knows we are here and knows what we do." The fact that donations are not rolling in (as they appear to for other organizations) can be misinterpreted as a lack of community backing.

More than likely, what is lacking is adequate visibility and proactive donor identification and cultivation. Implementing a mission-minded marketing strategy means getting the message out to the community in creative and effective ways – special events, videos, web site, newspaper articles, better signage, better promotional materials, radio spots, speaking to civic groups, etc. While this is always a good plan of action, it is especially important in anticipation of a capital campaign.

Make sure the community you serve understands your mission. Keep clarifying and reiterating the mission and the organization's story (history, good stewardship and lives changed) everywhere and through every means – from materials to donor cultivation meetings to newspaper articles. The purpose of greater visibility is not to solicit pats on the back from the community, but to solicit significant donors who can give the organization large gifts.

While you are increasing visibility, make sure any special events are also mission-minded. Donors, particularly major donors, have plenty of opportunities for entertainment, socializing and elaborate events. Ensure that your special event is not just one more soiree. Tie the mission to the event in a creative and uplifting way. Donors should not leave thinking only, "That was a great event!" but rather, "That is a great organization!" Relate the great accomplishments of the organization thematically with any speakers, venues, decor, audio/visual presentations, gifts, recognition and so on. Give major donors every opportunity possible to understand and care about the important work of your nonprofit.

RECOGNIZING AND ILLUMINATING DISTINCTIVENESS

Once you have identified prospective donors who care about the kind of work you do, it is time to demonstrate your distinctiveness. How is your nonprofit uniquely positioned, skilled and capable of serving others? If you were asked to give three examples of "lives changed," would you be able to share recent anecdotal evidences in a compelling manner? Yes, materials are helpful, but donors have probably heard those examples and read those quotes. They need to hear what happened last month, last week, today ...

Good cultivation can make friends of acquaintances, turn friends into regular donors, and bring regular donors up to a new level of major giving. Never move too far away from the mission in cultivation. Whatever method or means you use should always have the mission as its true North.

MONEY-MINDED VS. MISSION-MINDED CULTIVATION

Money-motivated fundraising will never be as potent and effectual as mission-minded money raising. At the same time, no development plan can overcome a shortfall in the basics of establishing and maintaining donor trust. In addition to a meaningful mission (not in word, but in deed), organizations must be able to prove their effectiveness, have a proven record of financial stewardship, and treat their donors with respect and appreciation.

Once the basics are in place, a mission-minded strategy for identifying and cultivating donors will open doors for more monetarily-meaningful fundraising solicitations (translation: big money).

BEST PRACTICES

Ensure every board meeting starts with five minutes of pure mission and vision, not just business.

Mary Murawski
Presbyterian Children's Services (St. Louis, Mo.)

Our Executive Director meets with new Board members six months into their first term. They begin with a discussion of our mission and what has 'surprised' the individual about the organization. It evolves into a detailed discussion regarding the volunteer's experiences as well as suggestions for improvement. The meetings conclude with discussion of the 'best ways they feel they can serve the organization.' The six-month timeframe is a key component to the interviews' success. Board members have had an opportunity to 'get their feet wet,' but also have the ability to be quite objective.

Maggie K. Schoepski
Ronald McDonald House (Rochester, Minn.)

We develop an inexpensive brochure/pamphlet as an annual report to share our story. It includes testimonials and financial data. It's a nice document that board members can use to share a passionate, compelling story. It's another way for us to show how the money is spent wisely.

Barbara Pauly
Arkansas Prostate Cancer Foundation (Little Rock, Ark.)

Demonstrating honest and ethical behavior in all situations goes a long way toward building donor relations and long-term commitments to the organization.

Gary M. Bernstein
Jewish Community Center (Louisville, Ky.)

Don't forget the people! You might have a great organization built around a great mission, but it's the people who bring meaning to the mission. So, when people start walking out the door, don't wonder how much it's going to cost to replace them, worry about what it is going to take to keep the ones who remain. For those remaining, find out more about them: likes and dislikes about their job, career aspirations and how their talents are being used, how they feel about the organization and their work schedule, and how they feel about their development so they are promotable and more marketable.

Lamech Mbise
Junior Achievement, Inc. (Colorado Springs, Colo.)

Women who are receiving medical assistance have done a video to show how important funding has been to them. This video was used as a promotional tool to ask for other donors to help support maternal and child health.

Susan Heilman
Wisconsin Child Care Improvement Project (Hayward, Wis.)

The endowment chair sponsors a lunch or other meeting with donor families and participants.

Unsigned

The core of success is the true spirit of excitement about the excellence and effectiveness of your program. You have to believe in what you are doing to be successful at it. That excitement spills over into all that you do. I am motivated to create a positive experience and an atmosphere of fun and energy for anyone who walks through our doors – be they million-dollar donors or complete strangers.

Kelley Barnes
National Dance Institute of New Mexico (Santa Fe, N.M.)

CHAPTER 2
PERSONALIZED CULTIVATION

Never fall into a trap of viewing donor information as purely administrative. Well-gathered and diligently maintained donor and prospective donor information is like a map to buried treasure (quite literally). Make sure the whole staff places a high value on donor details and data recording. When it comes to strengthening and broadening a donor's commitment to the organization, donor information is priceless.

The more information and the more extensive your research, the greater the potential for building something extraordinary. As it is with setting pylons for construction, so it is with donor research and information handling – dig deeper to build higher. Of course, the inverse is also true. When it comes to demolishing donor loyalty and razing relationships, what you don't know can hurt you.

One consultant tells a fundraiser's nightmare that came true. His organization maintained different donor lists. Development had one. Volunteers had another. Information was shared, but there was no fail-safe process in place, no common network to tie everything together in real time. Information from development would make its way to the women's auxiliary eventually, but not in time to steer clear of this car wreck.

As soon as the director of development saw the donor's face, he knew something was wrong – very wrong. This was a major donor with a major complaint. He had a longstanding and generous giving record and here he was, in the office, red in the face, and ready to blow a gasket. He held in his hand a beautiful invitation to a "Sweetheart's Event" sponsored by the women's auxiliary. It had reached him at his new address on time – no problem there. But the invitation was addressed to his deceased wife, not his current wife.

The donor had assumed that his strong connection with the organization merited enough familiarity to avoid such an offense. To the donor, it was not simply an administrative oversight; it demonstrated a deficiency in the donor/non-profit relationship.

The lesson can never be overstated: Know your donors and maintain donor information as the treasure that it is. Make sure good administrative systems are in place. Keep donor information up-to-date and all in one networked system. Finally, ensure that the information is well-managed with sound gatekeeping policies in place.

When it comes to soliciting major donors for large gifts, donor information is dynamite that can be used to blow open doors of opportunity or blow up in your face.

"WELL, WHAT DO YOU KNOW?"

Some people say it is not what you know, but whom you know. In fundraising, it is not just what you know or whom you know, it is what you know about whom.

So, what do you know about your donors? What information should be collected and maintained to cultivate important donor relationships more effectively for the purpose of soliciting gifts? First, get the basics: name (include salutation and documentation preferences such as Mr., Miss, Ms., Dr., Jr., III, etc.), addresses (also e-mail), phone (include home, work, cell and fax) family names, special dates and so on. But do not stop there.

KEEP UP WITH PERIPHERAL INFORMATION TOO:

- How did the donor first connect with the organization?
- Who was the donor's first contact?
- What is the donor's giving record?

Information that is particularly important for successful cultivation includes:

- Financial streams (inheritance, entrepreneur, inventor of Velcro®, etc.)
- Hobbies (and related specifics such as favorite sports team, favorite artist, etc.)
- Clubs and associations
- Hometown
- Alma mater
- Any other pertinent information picked up along the way

Good information gathering is motivated by a desire to get to know the donor so you can ask for the right-sized gift at the right point in time. The more you know about your donors, the more you can tailor your cultivation and solicitation to their tastes and preferences. But remember this good rule of thumb: Never make notations or include information that you would not want the donor to read.

DONOR INFORMATION AS A TOOL FOR CULTIVATION

When collecting contact information, be sure to include the donor's preference: phone or face-to-face, e-mail or snail mail, fax or FedEx, home or office, day or night. The more convenient and pleasant you can make your cultivation connections, the better.

With each cultivation contact or visit, keep track of any related giving. If every time Mrs. Watkins receives a newsletter, the organization receives a check, consider asking her if an automatic transfer every quarter would be a convenience. If Mr. Lee has been a regular supporter for two years (revealed through the donor report generated from your one seamless network), consider asking him for a major gift during the next campaign.

From there, dial up your cultivation connections until you feel it is appropriate to ask Mr. Lee about his interest in planned giving. How will you know when it is appropriate? A sixth sense for fundraising is good, but a long print-out of donor cultivation connections will help give you the confirmation you need to set up an appointment. A short list of only three impersonal connections (two special events and a lunch) means that more relationship building is probably in order before you ask for a major gift.

Keep track of any information that may be meaningful later on or under different circumstances. Did he say something about naming opportunities? Keep that on record for the next capital campaign. Did she say that her new book was coming out next month? Make a note to recognize her accomplishment. Mine all your donor conversations for gold nuggets that can be heated and molded into beautiful works of philanthropic giving.

USING TECHNOLOGY TO GATHER AND MAINTAIN INFORMATION

Index cards once were considered cutting-edge tools. Now there are more donor management systems than there are donors – or at least it can feel that way when you begin investigating options.

Fundraising software allows organizations to collect data more easily, manage it more effectively, and sort it a multitude of ways for a variety of purposes. Start with what you need and find software to fit the bill rather than purchase software because it does everything but slice and dice. (Actually you will need it to slice and dice.)

If you need five functions, do not buy expensive software that does 35. On the other hand, do not settle for inexpensive software that does not do everything you need it to do now, even if it has potential for expansion. Donor details are diamonds in the rough for soliciting big gifts. Manage them well.

When it comes to searching for hidden treasure, a map is only valuable if it is accessible, legible and accurate. So it is with donor information. Good data collection, entry and maintenance should always be valued for its important role in cultivation and, in due time, for successful major-gift solicitations.

BEST PRACTICES

Do not be intimidated by technology.

Kimberly Brown
Cho-Yeh Camp and Conference Center (Livingston, Tex.)

Capture as much information as soon as possible to avoid database-related problems.

Diane Creed
American Diabetes Association (Southbury, Conn.)

Use a data sort to identify highest-potential donors or constituent giving over time and more recently.

Dorothy Witte
Illinois State University (Normal, Ill.)

In many cases, appreciation is your best way of cultivating future donors. At one institution we were looking for creative ways to engage and interact with our military alumni. To do so, we instituted a donor program where once a year we mailed a personalized "Military Salute" to all our military alums. It recognized their service to our country. No solicitation or ask was involved in the salute, but the response both in total gifts and total dollars was tremendous.

Brett Blackwelder, MHSA
Hartsook Companies, Inc. (Kansas City, Mo.)

When meeting with donors and potential donors, especially seniors, I have found they share very important information in the last few minutes of the visit. This has taught me to listen carefully and watch for cues that, even though I think the visit might be about over, tell me it really isn't. More than once I have learned a key piece of information that helped tie the entire conversation together and have been thankful I waited those extra few minutes.

Jeff Jantz
Greencroft Foundation (Goshen, Ind.)

We establish pen-pal partnerships between children, our volunteers and corporate sponsors to generate awareness, prospects and connections.

Carleen Rhodes, CFRE
Minnesota Children's Museum (St. Paul, Minn.)

Do not be intimidated by foundations. Build and cultivate relationships with them and their program officers the same way you build and cultivate relationships with individual donors. Get to know their interests. Go out of your way to meet program officers and stay in touch regularly. Send them pieces of work they'd be interested in seeing, or summarize information you've uncovered that reinforces their interests. Respect them. Communicate with them and share with them. Build an informal partnership that benefits you both.

Marc Levin
The Alan Guttmacher Institute (New York, N.Y.)

Keep in continual contact with your campaign committee. Every single letter from our campaign chair mentions the donor by name. Personalize and complement. Thirty-seven committee members were very involved over a year and a half. We raised more money because we showed we genuinely cared. What they did led to friendly competition to improve each other. Also, we received in-kind media donations from leading newspapers and public relations firms.

Georgeanne Bassett
University of North Carolina (Chapel Hill, N.C.)

An article recently ran following a public-awareness event. I sent copies to donors no longer living in the area, letting them know what our organization was up to – and to remind them of their relationship with the organization.

Virginia Stallworth
Memphis Child Advocacy Center (Memphis, Tenn.)

When cultivating major gift relationships, learn to ask and listen. Offer open-ended questions that allow donors to declare their interests and positions then build on those offerings as the visit unfolds. If your speaking takes more than a quarter of the conversation's total time, you've spoken too much.

Matt Beem, MPA, CFRE
Hartsook Companies, Inc. (Kansas City, Mo.)

Put prospects on a spreadsheet and assign them a code in your fundraising software. This allows you to develop individual cultivation, solicitation and appreciation plans for each prospect. You can closely track their activity and place a priority on the area of development that provides the largest return for your organization.

Alex Burden, CFRE
Hartsook Companies, Inc. (Kansas City, Mo.)

For database analysis, we look for three types of donors: active, current and lapsed. Our strategies for addressing these people are based on their needs. The active people have a continual, ongoing relationship with us and we work hard to maintain that. Our current people are those who have not given in the past two years. For these, we send specialized mailings quarterly to keep them informed and spark their interest in the Institute.

Unsigned

Use your board in major donor cultivation, expanding resources and tapping into their connections.

Stacey Dickson
Harvesters-The Community Food Network (Kansas City, Mo.)

CHAPTER 3
CREATIVE CULTIVATION

Creative cultivation means using the talents, resources and specific mission of your organization to produce new methods and mediums for cultivation. It is very likely that your largest donors also are making charitable contributions to other organizations. Nonprofits that mostly give tours for cultivation, send only notes and pictures for appreciation, and hand out plaques for recognition can end up with donors who have "been there, done that, got the photo."

Go ahead and get colorful and creative outside the ordinary lines of conventional cultivation. Professional photos are nice, but what about a framed artist's rendering of the building named in his family's honor? A note of appreciation from the development director is important, but what about a note from one of the families served by your organization?

When you think recognition, remember that "plaque" is also the hard stuff that accumulates if not removed. Why cause build up on your donors' walls when you could present them with a small bronze sculpture of a mother and child – or whatever best embodies your organization's mission?

CREATIVE CONSIDERATION

It is through the generosity of interested donors that nonprofits continue to serve others. Consequently, organizations have become fairly proficient at saying, "thank you." And as important as that is (and it is hugely important), creative cultivation should take you beyond "thank you" to "What can we do for you?" To rephrase a famous admonition, "Ask not what your donors can do for you (as an organization); ask what you can do for your donors."

Maybe Mr. and Mrs. Major Donor do not really want to be presented with another boxed gift. Instead, what about hosting a dinner in their honor? Include a respected author (musician, artist, educator, elected official, sports personality, etc. – someone you know the couple would be interested in meeting) to the intimate gathering. Have the honorees invite two other couples (preferably two not already affiliated with the nonprofit) and celebrate their special relationship with the organization.

First identify the interests, passions and pursuits of your donors, and then consider how your organization might advance their dreams and aspirations. Reciprocating generosity through creative consideration (being helpful in addition to being thankful) is a wonderful way to strengthen donor relationships.

BUILD INTEREST BY USING CREATIVITY TO STAY IN TOUCH

Good communication is also a key to cultivation. Newsletters serve as a regular touch point, so make sure they are having an impact. E-newsletters (used more and more by nonprofits) should have the same "reach-out-and-touch-a-donor" objective. (Just make sure you know which donors prefer receiving hard-copy newsletters and oblige them.)

The purpose of the newsletter is to build major-gift relationships with donors and potential donors. It is not an in-house organ for the nonprofit. Focus any stories about staff on building credibility and donor trust. A story about a staff member who has just received a related degree or award – news-worthy. A story about a staff member who has just returned from a trip to Disney World – not news-worthy. The newsletter should be personal in tone, but professional in content.

Keep readers up-to-date on the organization's recent achievements, campaign gifts and progress, or meaningful "thank yous" from clients and client success stories. Also include a short, educational box about giving opportunities in every newsletter. Feature fundraising issues such as bequests, in-kind gifts, gifts of stock and insurance, and so on. Always end with a name, number and e-mail address if readers have more questions about the monthly giving topic.

Be especially creative when sending birthday and greeting cards. Does your organization work with children? Have them draw or paint pictures to include with cards or even have the children stamp-design the cards themselves. Have the children record the "Happy Birthday" song ("Happy Birthday, Mrs. Watkins …") on a CD and send it along with the card. Is a donor undergoing surgery? Flowers and a get-well card are great, but what about adding a few magazines related to the donor's hobbies and interests?

Of course, the better you know your donors, the more creative and personal you can be in your gestures. Always err toward prudence and propriety, but if you know a donor loves pistachios (and you should know), then a bag of those would be a better drop-off gift than another logo mug.

The goal is not to shower donors with gifts and cards; it is to demonstrate genuine appreciation. It is to acknowledge that the organization not only knows when a donor gives and how much he gives, but why he gives. It is to show that the organization knows the donor and sees him as an individual and not a walking (albeit well-appreciated) ATM. And it is an effective way of ensuring a successful major-gift solicitation when the time is right.

DRAW DONORS CLOSER INTO THE ORGANIZATION

One of the greatest ways to build interest in a nonprofit is to draw donors closer into the life of the organization. Whenever circumstances bring a donor to your facility, make sure to introduce them to staff members and program directors. Train everyone to understand beforehand the value of these brief, but important introductions.

Ask program directors and the people closest to the organization's mission to write donor thank-you notes and include updates on new programs or describe the benefit of a new capital addition, etc. Make sure they include pictures and anecdotes that showcase the mission in action.

Encourage donors to participate in the life of the organization whenever possible. Invite them to use their skills, talents and connections (not just their money) to enhance the work of the nonprofit.

Donors are under no obligation to give money to your organization. Thankfully, they have chosen to do so. Something about the organization's mission matters to them. Use these connections to create a better environment for major-gift solicitations down the road.

By continuing to demonstrate real interest in your donors through creative and sincere cultivation, you will undoubtedly increase your major donors' interest in the organization and their major gifts to the organization.

BEST PRACTICES

We've made an effort to invite all our capital campaign major donors in to see the completed building. Our invitation was a plastic hard hat, mailed in a box, which invited them in a month before the building was done. They thought the invitation creative enough that it piqued their interest and (they) came in record numbers.

Unsigned

We send newsletters and correspond with our gift annuity donors every time there is a rate change but we look for a reason to reach out to them at least twice a year. We try to make our correspondence personal, special and memorable. I always remember birthdays with a card, personal note, and a chocolate candy bar bearing the 'Happy Birthday' sentiment. For about two dollars we've made an impression they remember and look forward to each year.

Judie List Sweeney, CFRE
Disabled American Veterans National Headquarters
(Cincinnati, Ohio)

We solicit previous memorial donors in May and June for Mother's Day, Father's Day and Memorial Day. We plant a flower garden in their memory on our campus.

Dave Foubert
Otterbein Homes (Lebanon, Ohio)

We send donors a jar of honey each year. Our president raises bees, so the connection between the organization and leadership makes a strong statement and serves as a great reinforcer.

Matthew Ruffner
The Leadership Institute (Arlington, Va.)

We introduced our capital campaign to all staff with a play produced by volunteers from throughout our organization. It spoofed the TV show Gilligan's Island (complete with our actors' faces popping up instead of the real Gilligan, Skipper and the rest at the beginning of a clip from the TV show). It was fully scripted and costumed, and served as a fun entrée to the campaign. Near the end, two employees spoke from their heart about the importance of the campaign and encouraged involvement.

Tim M. Ipema
Unity (Unity Village, Mo.)

We have turned away from paid premiums and instead thank donors with 'Salon Evenings.' We bring in a writer or artist to their home for an intimate evening of 25 to 50 people (donors plus their select guests). The result: we spend much less on the thank-you gifts than before – and it has paid off with larger donations to our organization. We do this about five times a year as a special event for those in our 'inner circle' of donors. It's much more fun than packing up mugs!

Keri Healey
Washington Commission for the Humanities (Seattle, Wash.)

Invite donors in for visitors' day. Posters and pictures are placed around the office that visually tell the organization's story. Visitors are shown a seven-minute video. A core member oversees the tour and gives a testimonial of why they have committed to one year as a mentor and/or tells success stories related to how they've touched the life of a child.

Pamela Joy Pratt, CFRE
City Year (Detroit, Mich.)

We put our 1,000 largest donors on a special contact list and schedule. We invite them to special events. The average gift increased 25 percent; we've raised additional monies from this group.

Greg Lee
The Salvation Army (St. Paul, Minn.)

Besides our regular business cards, we have special cards that include our organization's contact information on one side (but not the person's name) and, on the reverse, a picture of a big table and a simple invitation for people to stop by and see Second Harvest firsthand. We encourage our entire staff to distribute these cards. We have found it very empowering for our staff and a successful means of connecting with the community. Once a person takes us up on the offer to visit we direct them to the development office and begin the process of cultivation.

Jason Clark
Second Harvest Food Bank of the Inland Northwest
(Spokane, Wash.)

One of our board members was being sued by a former employee. When I called to remind him of his overdue donation (annual gift) he told me about his circumstances. I did not mention the gift, but instead rallied the troops, got him attorneys and consultants, and helped him with his legal problems. Again, I never mentioned the gift. Once his problems were resolved, he doubled the annual gift.

Tim Hall
Health Talents International, Inc. (Huntsville, Ala.)

Every month we circulate to our board a set of donor sheets: each individual who has given $250 or more. The members call the donor and say, 'Hi, I'm a volunteer board member...and thank you.' Then they listen to donors, and hear why they, the donors, care about our organization. Donors love it. The board loves it. Each board member hears five to 10 times a month how wonderful we are. That gives them great confidence when they ask for funds or represent our organization.

Gordon Durnan
South Muskoka Hospital Foundation (Bracebridge, Ontario)

CHAPTER 4
CULTIVATION THROUGH DONOR PARTICIPATION

TURN DONORS INTO OWNERS

Even the strongest work ethic in an employee (or in this case, a donor) runs a close second to the vested interest of a proprietor. Owners personally identify with the business. Every aspect of the organization, from brand to customer service and from production to distribution, matters to them on a gut level. They care and they carry the weight of current needs and future challenges with them everywhere they go. They are tireless in their efforts and uncompromising in their work.

Owners know that if they come across a good idea to build a better mousetrap, the idea will be implemented. Owners know that their efforts have a direct cause-and-effect relationship in the success of the organization. Owners never take time off without making sure the office knows where they can be reached. Owners are never indifferent to changes in the tax laws or economic downturns or anything that might affect business.

If only nonprofits could engender this kind of identification and sense of responsibility between donors and the organizations they support! With the right strategies, they can.

The first step is to change the culture of the organization from viewing donors as silent partners to seeing them as full-fledged shareholders. With this new outlook, begin to ask for feedback from your most significant donors.

Most organizations take the pulse of donors prior to a campaign. This is a smart and necessary strategy. But do not relegate donor interviews to a campaign assessment tool only. Asking donors for their opinions helps cultivate the relationship; it gives the organization an opportunity to hear new ideas from a different perspective.

One way to recognize whether a donor has been made to feel like one of the "owners" is to listen to what pronouns she uses. Does she ask, "How did you do on that grant?" What you want to hear is, "How did we do?" You will know donor loyalty is on the rise when you hear more "we," "us" and "ours" in conversations. Be sure to model this language in all your newsletters and correspondence, as well.

As donors experience a greater personal connection to the organization, you will be able to ask them for larger gifts.

FRIEND RAISING

Another way to use active involvement to bolster donor loyalty and breed major giving is to meet with small groups of like-minded donors and facilitate opportunities for them to network and build relationships with one another.

Are there educators among your constituents? Form a small think-tank for programming suggestions. Are any of your donors from the same alma mater? Consider a special event where they can invite other alumni for a program tour and presentation. Put the university's logo on the invitation and make the "suggested attire" the school's colors and mascot. Identify and begin to cultivate these prospective donors for future solicitations.

Do not expect donors to feel a strong affinity to your organization just because their gifts are "greatly appreciated." Make their connections with the nonprofit relational, even familial. Plenty of worthy nonprofits would "appreciate" a donor's million-dollar gift. Help your donors form a special loyalty, identity and association with your organization.

OUT OF 'SITE,' OUT OF MIND

When was the last time you had each of your major donors on site for a visit? Make site visits special, memorable events. Take donors behind the scenes. Arrange for them to speak with the people who serve the organization day in and day out. Do not simply tour the facility; let donors experience the work that is accomplished there.

Nothing can be said or read that will convey the importance of the organization's mission better than seeing the mission in action. On-site visits, coupled with the culture of "donor as owner," may even prompt inspired questions: "Are we about to outgrow this space? What does the future hold for acquiring the property next door? The owner of that lot and I happen to belong to the same association." How motivated do you think a donor will be to serve, support and solicit gifts for a campaign that she helped prompt through her questions and concern? Look for every opportunity to generate donor interest and ideas and then move mountains to help see those ideas implemented.

OTHER IMPORTANT 'ASKS'

Most fundraisers are really beginning to get it. They know they have to ask for a gift. They know that they cannot wait for donors to feel particularly generous and moved to write a check without being given a special invitation to do so. But there are other "asks" that fundraisers should be taking advantage of for money-raising purposes.

We have talked about asking donors for input and suggestions, but what about asking for specific professional counsel. Since most major donors have acquired a lot of experience, skill and wisdom along the way to achieving financial prominence, it makes sense to utilize this storehouse of information for the organization's benefit. Not only is it practical, but seeking someone's "professional opinion" is another way of saying, "We recognize and respect your expertise."

Just remember, if you ask questions, you will get answers. Be willing to listen and learn. When you ask questions, you also will get more questions. Soliciting donors for information means putting the organization's cards on the table. Make sure you are prepared to answer all questions honestly and confidently. Should a donor ask a question you cannot answer, make a note of it and get back to her with an answer as soon as possible.

Increasing donor involvement through participation and seeking advice are legitimate means for strengthening donor relationships. And the greater a donor's loyalty and identification with the organization, the more likely it is that he or she will want to give a gift of significance.

BEST PRACTICES

When recruiting volunteers, understand what it is they are looking for – a short-term project or something long-term such as a Board position. Be up front with the specific needs of your organization while still being respectful of their personal lives. Present an opportunity that meets both of your needs with specifics such as the number of calls to make (never more than five unless you find a pro), the time commitment, and, most important, their financial support! Give them realistic expectations and obtainable goals. Don't sugar-coat the work that needs to be done.

Chris Kramer
Science Center of Iowa (Des Moines, Iowa)

We sponsor the USU/Community Associates, an organization of university faculty, staff and community leaders, including University President Kermit L. Hall. Its members, who are invited to join and pay $75 to belong, meet twice a year – once on campus and once in the community. They discuss and explore issues of campus and community importance and interest. Our gatherings include a reception, a display and a presentation by one of our colleges, departments or businesses in town. They end with student or community entertainment. This is pure relationship building and cultivation – no solicitation occurs. At the same time, many members are donors; those who aren't usually become donors eventually.

Jan Appuhn, CFRM
Utah State University (Logan, Utah)

When visiting with a planned giving prospect, broaching a general discussion of the ever-changing estate tax laws can help identify which type of planned gift is best for the donor while also yielding valuable information on the size of their estate.

Eileen Brown, JD
Hartsook Companies, Inc. (Kansas City, Mo.)

Invite foundation givers to not only shake your hand and give the check, but to participate in the actual program they support. Example: Foundation members attended a day of 'Sprout Camp' and helped plant new things in the Children's Garden.

Mary McFadden Craft
Daniel Stowe Botanical Garden (Belmont, N.C.)

As a personalized cultivation strategy, we offer potential major donors 'hard-hat tours' of soon-to-be opened facilities or regular tours of existing facilities. This helps them envision or see what the facility is about and to gain a deeper understanding of the good that will occur, or is occurring, there. We include visits along the way with people who deliver or benefit from our care so our visitors can share in their passion and excitement.

Manon O'Connor
Fletcher-Allen Health Care (Burlington, Vt.)

We invite donors to cultural lunches where food is provided by our extremely diverse population of students.

Jessica Smith
Project Regina (Minneapolis, Minn.)

We recruit a group of community leaders and business people to spend a portion of their day with a 'disability.' It has been a great awareness event.

Shalle Wolff
The Bethphage Foundation (Omaha, Neb.)

As an international micro-lending organization, we regularly invite donors to travel and see our work firsthand. These "Insight Trips" are an amazing and often life-changing experience for our donors, many of whom have never seen real poverty. We prepare customized 'storybooks' to capture the stories and photos that summarize the most compelling client visits. Volunteers put the photos and stories together in a simple format and create a beautiful cover. We print them in color on our own printer. This makes a great post-trip gift and gives us a reason to get together with donors and their friends to talk about the impact our work is having around the world.

Wendy Cox
Opportunity International (Oak Brook, Ill.)

Use community-wide strategic planning (headed up by a facilitator) to bring together colleagues and collaborators for mutual benefit. It brings organizations together who previously saw themselves solely as competitors to make significant mutual gain. An example: The cancer services task force has 19 service providers who met monthly for six months. They recently raised $350,000 in new funding for cancer.

Unsigned

BEST PRACTICES FOR PRODUCTIVE COMMUNICATION

Get development officers in the field and away from their desk, away from the day-to-day paperwork. Get them out where they can talk to people, learn more about your mission, communicate and connect.

Bert Armstrong
Methodist Home for Children (Raleigh, N.C.)

The best ideas are common property.

Seneca, Epistles
Roman dramatist, philosopher and politician
(5 BC – 65 AD)

What are you communicating to your past, current and prospective donors? Regardless of whether your organization has a strategic plan for communication or the development director picks up the phone and schedules donor visits "when there is time" donors are receiving a message. Is it the right one? What message have you communicated to your donors in the past month? The past six months? The past year?

DEVELOPMENT DIRECTOR, WHERE ARE YOU?

As a general rule, development directors need to be out of the office doing the real work of fundraising. Cell phones, voice mail and palm pilots make this more doable today than ever. You can easily stay accessible while you are out there communicating your organization's message for the ultimate purpose of asking donors for big gifts.

If you want to measure the success of fundraisers, call them. If they answer readily, whom are they talking to about the mission and impact of your nonprofit? Good fundraisers are always on the go – seeking out new prospects, communicating with current supporters, sharing their message through public speaking opportunities, conducting strategy meetings, etc. Oftentimes, CEO's and executive directors expect their fundraisers to put in an 8-to-5 day in the office, but that is exactly the wrong attitude. They should put in the hours, but maximize that time with prospects or donors according to their schedules.

COMMUNICATE, COMMUNICATE AND COMMUNICATE SOME MORE

Of course, communication should also come in the form of regular monthly newsletters filled and overflowing with anecdotal stories, interesting pictures and opportunities to become more involved in the life of the organization. E-mailed press releases and faxed news articles should be automatically forwarded to all major donors. Current and potential donors should see something about the organization or hear something from your office at least two or three times a month.

Some institutions have learned the hard way that when it comes to fundraising and their constituents, absence does not make the heart grow fonder. A hundred-year-old college-preparatory high school had kept limited information on decades of graduates. When it came time to renovate the campus facilities, the school looked to many of its very successful alumni for gifts. While the institution eventually met its multimillion-dollar goal, the initial campaign year was spent listening to disgruntled constituents ask, "Why is this the first time I've seen or heard from you since graduation?" A lot of fence mending and consoling had to take place before solicitors could even think about asking for gifts.

Use good communication skills on a regular basis – a long time before your organization begins discussing a campaign. Do not be like the man who, after 25 years of marriage, was shocked to see his wife packed up and leaving him. "I had no idea anything was wrong," he said. "How can you think there's nothing wrong," the wife replied. "It's obvious you don't love me." "Don't love you? Don't love you? Didn't I tell you I loved you the day we got married? And didn't I say that if that ever changed, I'd let you know?"

Let donors know, now, that you are interested in them. Keep communicating the mission and achievements of the organization on an ongoing basis. Make sure you are communicating the exact message you want donors to receive, and do it before they consider "leaving" and certainly well before launching a campaign.

When interacting with prospects, ask open-ended rather than closed-ended questions. You'll learn more about a donor, for instance, if you ask, "Where have you traveled in your life?" than if you ask, "Did you take a vacation last summer?" If you talk more than 25 percent of the time when visiting, you've spoken too much.

Matt Beem, MPA, CFRE
Hartsook Companies, Inc. (Kansas City, Mo.)

CHAPTER 5
"WHAT WE HAVE HERE IS A PLAN TO COMMUNICATE"

In the 1967 movie, "Cool Hand Luke," the captain of Road Prison 36 mocks the prisoners' attempts at escape as "failure to communicate." Later in the movie, when prison guards close in on Luke (played by a young Paul Newman), he mimics the captain and recycles the line. "What we have here is a failure to communicate." Obviously, what they had was not so much a miscommunication as a miscalculation. The prisoners were listening. They just did not like what they heard.

When it comes to raising money for your organization, it is necessary to have an intentional plan for clear communication. It is not enough to know what you want to say. It is more important to know what your donors want to hear – or need to hear – and to get that information to them in a convincing and impressionable fashion.

Simply saying more, more often, is not an efficient or effective plan. Frequency and repetition are important ingredients in getting your message across – both to in-house staff and volunteers and outside the organization to donors and a wider community audience. It is essential that you convey the right message in a compelling and memorable way.

Persuasive communication is not manipulation. You must first face and overcome any idea that your job is to talk donors into doing anything they do not want to do. You cannot – and should not try to – make them give money to your organization. Nobody wants to give money away! They do, however, want to make a difference in the world, and your organization very well may be the means through which they choose to do it.

You have probably heard the old adage, "You can lead a horse to water, but you can't make him drink." Well, you may not be able to make him drink, but you can certainly salt his oats. In other words, you are not pushing donors into anything. You are salting their oats with factual information, compelling needs and life-changing opportunities. You are creating a thirst for contributing major gifts to your organization.

So what kind of communication can bring about this kind of mouth-watering generosity? It is more than having your facts and figures in place, although that is essential, and it is more than having stacks of four-color glossy materials, although that is an added bonus. Good communication starts with a powerful message and a credible messenger (either you or others, or even media) who can deliver that message with potency.

WHAT DID HE SAY?

Have you ever heard – or more accurately – have you ever seen a speaker take the stage and hold a room in rapt attention. It is not unusual for someone not in attendance to ask later, "What did he say?" and get an odd answer, "I don't remember what he said, but the way he said it was outstanding!" What has happened here is that the speaker's message and persona has been imparted as much as, or more than, information has been presented.

What this means for fundraisers is that you must not only plan strategically for how you will communicate your organization's message, but diligently and methodically plan what that overall message should be. Promotional materials, case statements, radio spots, billboards, news articles, newsletters, phone calls, e-mail, web sites, etc. are only conduits for delivering a message. You must first take the time to construct your message in a manner that is clear, convincing and memorable.

C.L.E.A.R. Communication

Your message is more than your mission statement. It is the lasting impression of the organization that you leave with donors and the community. Is your organization "stridently professional" or "Generation Next casual"? Is it "progressive and edgy" or "steeped in tradition"? Everything from the font types used on brochures and web sites to the language used in radio spots and case statements should support a seamless message: "This is who we are. This is what we do." Your message should then be communicated consistently in whatever venue you use to build visibility and connect with donors (newsletters, face-to-face visits, press releases, television spots, etc.).

A "C.L.E.A.R." Message is:

- Compelling – It has an emotional connection.
- Lasting – It is memorable. It sticks with you.
- Efficient – It hits the right target.

- Accurate – It is truthful and genuine.
- Repeatable – It can be recycled from venue to venue.

TURN YOUR NORMAL INTO NEWS

An old commercial recommended that, "If you want to capture someone's attention, whisper." Many of the best methods for gaining visibility are counter-intuitive.

Once you have clarified your message (the impression you want to present to the world, the community, prospective donors and major donors), consider creative ways to have others get your message out for you.

For example, check your city's paper for the journalists covering your nonprofit's sector (education, the arts, religion, sports, etc.) and read their articles. Now, remember the importance of cultivation? What about bringing a journalist to your facility for a tour? Be ready with some human-interest stories or campaign highlights that might work for articles. Is there a story already in the news that could be easily tied to your organization? Offer to provide a quote whenever it is needed for related stories.

The word "broadcast" was originally the verb used to describe how farmers sowed seed. They would cast it out far and wide. They knew that their hard work of broadcasting would eventually result in a harvest. Once you have evaluated and clarified the impression you want to have on donors, prospective donors and the community – a plan for C.L.E.A.R. communication – you can be more deliberate, confident and creative in disseminating your message.

BEST PRACTICES

Good stories in the media create and build your organization's credibility, as well as interest, excitement and trust. When an event or occurrence is truly special — such as when we met our challenge grant well before deadline — we call a press conference. The secret is to have a story worth telling and something important enough that the entire community will notice and care. Save a press conference for the big announcement, not for every little bit of news.

Jean Meeks
Academy of Music Theater, Inc. (Lynchburg, Va.)

Develop, test and refine a crisis-communications plan to protect your organization's reputation. Include identified and trained spokespeople (lead, first and second alternates); situation-analysis procedures; internal and external protocols for first notice, first hour, first day, ongoing, closure and follow up; anticipated situations and possible responses; and standard background materials. Keep a copy in the office and another with each of the key people who will implement the plan.

Ron Fredman, APR
Hartsook Companies, Inc. (Kansas City, Mo.)

We are very dedicated and 'strict' about holding our weekly development meetings.

Hillary Nather
Boys Town National Research Hospital (Omaha, Neb.)

I meet with all committees once a month. It helps me to keep them engaged in the process so they're empowered.

Nancy Coffee
Greater Memphis Arts Council (Memphis, Tenn.)

Just because someone is an annual donor does not mean you contact them once a year! Be creative and communicate with them regularly. Use e-mail to provide continuous updates so donors can see how their gifts are making a difference.

Emily Aldrich Barbour
Hartsook Companies, Inc. (Raleigh, N.C.)

Make certain all departments communicate and run news releases and other public announcements past key people to ensure there are no concerns, changes or surprises.

Barbara Buoy-McCray
Catholic Relief Services (Baltimore, Md.)

Volunteers do 95 percent of our work. We publish a volunteer newsletter four times a year and have a volunteer recognition luncheon annually.

Gail Davis
Feed My People (St. Louis, Mo.)

Stay in touch with donors every month.

Rosalea Maher
Youth Emergency Services, Inc. (Omaha, Neb.)

Create a membership category for distant friends of your organization, those who have moved to other communities. Keep them engaged through a low-cost newsletter from the desk of the president or executive director. Ask other donors who know them to mention your organization's good work. Continue to invite them to events as if they lived in the area.

Lynn Hawks
Wichita Art Museum (Wichita, Kan.)

When it comes to quality coverage and media placement, the key is in building relationships with those who write or produce the stories. It is worth taking the time to get to know journalists and what they like to cover. They will appreciate your help in developing good story ideas and you won't waste their time with topics that are irrelevant to them. It also is in your interest to help 'frame' the story, article or broadcast in a favorable light for your organization and to be certain all information is accurate and complete. Further, it is useful if you can tell your management team and trustees in general terms what they might expect and when.

JoAnne Vose
The Forsyth Institute (Boston, Mass.)

Make friends and discover their visions.

Carol Mack
South Side Day Nursery (St. Louis, Mo.)

Communication, education and connection drive our annual employee-giving campaign. We keep our employees, and the employees of the hospital we're affiliated with, apprised of events, grants and successes through a one-page newsletter e-mailed every two months. More important, through words and actions every day, we build and reinforce an attitude and environment of family and caring. Our employees buy into it and serve as advocates to their peers and the community.

Ray Domingue
Lourdes Foundation (Lafayette, La.)

CHAPTER 6
TARGETED
COMMUNICATION

COMMUNICATE WITH THE RIGHT PEOPLE

A small social service nonprofit deliberated over its need to raise $100,000 for an important community project. It was a noble cause, worthy of citywide support. Not surprisingly, one board member proposed taking the need directly to the public. "Let's get a thousand people to give a hundred dollars!" The idea of using a weighted-average formula to raise money is an old standby of nonprofits that have a limited understanding of the potential for major-gift fundraising.

A better mathematical method is to use the 20-80 rule. In most organizations, agencies, churches and clubs, 20 percent of the people do 80 percent of the work. The same goes for giving. In fact, the ratio is probably closer to 10-90.

If you understand that a small number of people (who have a large capacity to give financially to your organization) can meet the major portion of your fundraising goals, then you can target your communication to reach these people in a more efficient and effective manner.

Knowing that you will need to communicate your message to people of significant wealth means that you must be able to speak their language. While the wealthy are as varied and diverse as any other economic demographic, they still tend to have some things in common. They have a number of organizations vying for their time and resources; they are accustomed to quality and excellence; and they are not interested in giving their money away unless there is a very good reason to do so.

FACE-TIME

One-on-one cultivation, communication and solicitation of major donors are really the best means for today's non-profits to stay viable. Donors who have the ability to fund your organization generously will likely be very busy people. You must make the very best use of any face-time you have. Understanding the reason(s) why certain donors give will help you target your communication and use your time wisely.

In the book, "The Seven Faces of Philanthropy: A New Approach to Cultivating Major Donors," co-authors Karen Maru and Russ Alan Prince identify general motivations for giving and assign labels to donors who give for specific reasons. The seven donor descriptions include: Communitarian, Devout, Investor, Socialite, Altruist, Repayer and Dynast.

As you communicate with donors, learn to listen for clues to what prompts a particular donor to give. Look for insights into the passions and motivations of your donors so you can target your communication to suit their tastes. Here is a brief rundown of the seven donors.

THE COMMUNITARIAN

Communitarians believe philanthropy is a great way to improve the community. Since they are often business owners and civic leaders, they are most likely networked and can easily imagine (and may suggest) how a nonprofit's efforts can have a positive influence on other projects in the community. For Communitarians, doing "good" makes good sense.

THE DEVOUT

The Devout believe that doing good is, in a spiritual sense, the right thing to do. They consider their giving as giving to God and godly causes. The Devout virtually always give through their churches or through other religious groups.

THE INVESTOR

Investors believe that giving to the right cause is profitable. Affluent Investors usually have a greater interest in tax incentives than other types of philanthropists. They are more likely to want to pull in accountants and attorneys to discuss the details of a gift. They also tend to diversify their giving among several organizations.

THE SOCIALITE

Socialites believe that doing good deeds should be fun as well. They want to give to an organization where they will have opportunities to interact with friends and make new acquaintances. Socialites enjoy helping with galas and special events, but are not as interested in the day-to-day dealings of an organization. They tend to care about the arts and education.

THE ALTRUIST

Altruists do not have a strong desire to be recognized. Some even prefer anonymity. An Altruist believes that doing good and giving financially is a moral obligation. They derive pleasure simply from the act of giving and feel that it helps them to grow as a person.

THE REPAYER

Repayers believe that they have benefited from a particular institution or organization and feel a need to reciprocate. They want to express appreciation and thankfulness. Hospitals and universities are very often the beneficiaries of Repayers.

THE DYNAST

For Dynasts, generous giving is a family tradition. Dynasts usually have substantial inherited wealth and significant social connections. Naming opportunities are often important to Dynasts in order to maintain public name recognition.

The goal for major-gift fundraising is to garner the greatest support from the fewest number of donors. To do so, you must make your communication count. Remember that you are not selling a product, but you are communicating an opportunity for donors to achieve the satisfaction they are seeking. Once you know what motivates a donor to give, you can take aim, target your communication and, most important, hit the bull's-eye.

BEST PRACTICES

Before publicly promoting an event, we first send a targeted mailing to major donors and highly qualified prospects. The design and packaging of the save-the-date card and formal invitation speak of elegance and selectiveness; the special receptions for those recipients further reinforce exclusivity and status. This strategy often increases response to the 'higher-end tickets' for our events.

April Harris
University of Alabama-Huntsville (Huntsville, Ala.)

In restructuring our Board of Directors, we identified candidates of influence and affluence. We made a conscious decision to seek support from our community's leaders and to build a powerful Board. Not all candidates had a direct relationship with our organization at that point; all, however, did have a relationship with another member of our Board. We tailored cultivation activities to each prospect, led by a person with whom they were acquainted. The status of our Board membership helped secure commitments.

Melissa Steimer
Durham Western Heritage Museum (Omaha, Neb.)

There are a lot of elderly citizens on the Web. Assume they're online, looking for information when terminal illness strikes. Don't forget to communicate through the Internet with seniors.

Robert Mueller
Hospice of Louisville (Louisville, Ky.)

A luncheon recruited me to the board of the Community Medical Center. They paid a lot of attention to me, then followed through as promised.

Jane Walstrom, CFRE
St. Madeline Sophies Center (El Cajon, Calif.)

We have 36,000 students and 250,000 alumni – yet had never taken care of our database. We only had 20,000 records. We also had no experience within our people for building a database. It was a big challenge. We put ads in magazines and newspapers around the country saying, 'We're looking for you.' We sent letters to their last known address. We used e-mail and the Internet and outdoor advertising, asking people to contact us.

Custodio Pereira
MacKenzie University (Sao Palo, Brazil)

For youth organizations, don't forget your best salespeople are the youth who are playing ball, joining your troop or doing whatever it is you do. Encourage them to talk to their friends about how much fun they're having and to invite those friends to join in. Consider a recruiting contest where all who bring in someone get a patch or simple gift, and the top two or three receive something a little more significant. This same strategy works well with adults.

Wade M. Post
Nampa Babe Ruth, Inc. (Nampa, Idaho)

We find families who want to adopt orphans by presenting free informational meetings. It's essential that we advertise these meetings cost-effectively. To track what advertising works and what doesn't, I created a 'summary sheet': where the seminar was held, day of the week, time of day, where we placed the advertising, etc. I enter the results of the advertising on the same page: how many people attended, how many were ready to sign up for pre-adopt classes, how many calls we had from people who couldn't attend but wanted more information, and how attendees learned about the meeting. This lets me plan our future advertising more effectively.

Carole Lawrence
PLAN Loving Adoptions Now, Inc. (McMinnville, Ore.)

Work to involve more minority constituents and clients.

Patrick Frase
Franciscan Friars (Pulaski, Wis.)

Our first annual Gala Committee was comprised of newer philanthropists.

Ann Tubbs
Vera French Foundation (Davenport, Iowa)

Create Young Philanthropist Awards to encourage gifts of time, talent and treasure among the younger generation.

Sue Watts
St. Vincent Hospital (Green Bay, Wis.)

At a former place I worked, we provided luggage tags with the foundation name to conference attendees so they could keep track of their tote bags – and to have our name on something they'd use long after our conference.

Lynn Raney
Children's Hope International (St. Louis, Mo.)

CHAPTER 7
PERSONALIZE YOUR COMMUNICATION

Good communication is more than what you say. It is how you say it. It is how you deliver the information. As Marshall McLuhan illuminated in his classic work "Understanding Media," "the medium is the message." (By the way, McLuhan was the first to coin the term "media.") He explained that the extensions we choose to express ourselves (a hammer, a telephone, a paintbrush, a computer, a megaphone, etc.) go a long way in defining our message. They can enhance or detract, but they will always influence the message we want to communicate.

Professor Albert Mehrabian, PhD and Professor Emeritus of Psychology, UCLA, researched and developed the following statistical analysis for understanding effective communication. He concluded that:

- Seven percent of meaning is in the spoken word.
- Thirty-eight percent of meaning is in the way words are said.
- Fifty-five percent of meaning is in facial expressions and body language.

Even if you have heard this before, and even if you believe you understand the importance of nonverbal communication, are you sure you have incorporated this truth into your fundraising lifestyle? Have you considered how it relates to your cultivation and solicitation efforts? Have you thought about the nuance necessary for voice mail, e-mail, letters and phone conversations? Generally, any communication that reduces your efficiency by 55 percent has a higher threshold for misinterpretation.

As a rule of thumb, it is more difficult to convey true intent by e-mail than by phone, and harder to be clearly understood by phone than in person. When dealing with major donors, be careful with nonverbal communication. Make sure that you are passing along the right message with the right tone. Choose the right venue to deliver the right information. Solicitations, for example, are too important to attempt over the phone. These require a face-to-face meeting.

At the same time, ensure that you understand and properly utilize all 55 percent of your nonverbal communication when you are face to face with donors. Have you ever watched yourself ask for a gift? Try it. Pitch your solicitation in front of a mirror and see what you think. Maybe you have been confident that your solicitation is bold and convincing. You "know" this to be true because it sounds so convincing to you. But remember that this is only part of the story. Do your facial expressions and body language belie your well-chosen words?

Understanding your natural strengths and weaknesses in communication allows you to work on your weaknesses and maximize your strengths. Are you naturally funny and gregarious? Use it. Do you genuinely care about your organization's mission? Express it in a way that is personal and authentic. Are you gifted with technology? Incorporate a PowerPoint presentation. Are you technologically-challenged? Skip the PowerPoint and speak from the heart.

Either way, make sure to include specific examples of what your organization achieves in the lives of its constituents. It is more compelling to talk about one life changed (especially if a real-life story includes pictures and outcomes) than to say 100 people were helped last year.

Also learn to pick up on the 55 percent of nonverbal communication that your donors are sending to you. Never get so caught up in your own presentation that you miss the spark in your donor after you mention the educational aspect of the campaign. When you see it, stop in your tracks. As TV's Dr. Phil says, quoting his father, "Never miss a good opportunity to shut up." Key in on subjects that appear to raise a donor's interest. You will miss the silent clues for targeted communication if you underestimate the power of the unspoken message.

Personalizing your communication and paying attention to the other 55 percent of the conversation can mean a 100 percent increase in your fundraising potential.

BEST PRACTICES

We use student successes in newsletters, some of it autobiographical, to build interest, value and awareness.

Dawn Finley
Bynum School (Midland, Tex.)

I use the 'Starfish Story' with donors, prospects and others. Once upon a time, there was a little girl standing on the beach. As she stood on the shore, waves threw starfish onto the sand. As that happened, she threw them back, one after another. A man walked by and watched the little girl throwing the starfish into the water, one at a time. After watching her for a few minutes, he said, 'You know, what you're doing makes no sense. You can't possibly keep up with the waves. What you're doing makes no difference at all.' The little girl looked at the man. As she looked at him, another wave threw more starfish onto the beach. She picked one up and threw it back into the water. Then she looked back at the man and said, 'It made a difference to that one.' (Author unknown)

Barbara Foley
Emergency Nurses Care (Hollywood, Calif.)

Community leadership and involvement means networking!

Allison McElroy
Adult Development Center (Rogers, Ark.)

We produce an annual, four-color Thanksgiving mailing. Each year it varies. Sometimes it's an emotional piece from the perspective of a loved one whose family member was helped by our organization; other times it's a serious piece with a message on our organizations. Board members write personal notes to individuals they know; everyone receives a giving envelope and personal letter along with the mailing. A 4,000-piece mailing nets around $30,000.

Carma McKay
Rosehedge AIDS Housing (Seattle, Wash.)

We always ask for input from those we serve. We invite them to help us design better programs, and seek their advice on the effectiveness of those programs. Some of the input is formal and structured; much is informal. We also encourage them to discuss and write down their experiences. We then use those comments in marketing, news stories, fundraising and other outreach. For children, we obtain permission from their parents before using one of their comments.

Ranard Head
Boys & Girls Club of Covington County (Collins, Miss.)

Use creative voice mail – and have fun – to generate response. Put humor into your voice (and maybe a little guilt: 'You don't call, – you don't write'). It dramatically increases return calls.

Suzee Johnston
Advancing Philanthropy (Overland Park, Kan.)

We include a photo of one of our athletes, accompanied by their Special Olympics Oath, in all donor correspondence. The photos change with the time of year (and the competition that we are about to have). We receive many positive comments. With increasingly available and affordable technology such as color printers, it is very simple to create and update.

Sharon J. Couture
Special Olympics Florida (Clermont, Fla.)

Never forget your alumni's spouses. Keep them in the loop – for now and later. You miss the boat if you don't invite spouses to things, too. We had an alumnus turn 90 years old, so we sent a cherry pie with a huge card from the students. We knew his wife had been ill. We sent her a get-well card before we sent the birthday card and pie. It showed we cared.

Jill Belcher
New Mexico State University (Las Cruces, N.M.)

We were able to get former legislators to talk to the current legislators and members of Congress to help us bring in government money. The former legislators know all the right people. They don't get asked for much anymore, but they can be good lobbyists and supporters.

Jessica White
Jessica White Associates (Indianapolis, Ind.)

To raise awareness, build legitimacy, highlight success, show sound stewardship and recognize our supporters, we have created our first annual report. Photos and stories about our programs and the people we serve fill most of the document. We devoted one page to our financial highlights. By mail and in person, we are distributing it to donors, businesses, prospects and others. We also plan to put it on-line.

Deborah Walsh
Tri-County CAP, Inc. (Berlin, N.H.)

Incorporate Flash Macromedia into e-mails so PowerPoint presentations have sound, movement, etc.

Ronald Oyer
American Heart Association (St. Louis, Mo.)

CHAPTER 8
CAMPAIGN COMMUNICATION

Say It Like You Mean It

Fundraising, at its most basic, is a form of marketing and sales. Through a logical progression of communications and relationship building, you are strengthening awareness, interest, trust, trial and, ultimately, investment.

A strong message delivered strongly will connect you with and motivate your prospects – emotionally and intellectually. Well-crafted campaign-communications tools will reinforce that you are a smartly run organization with a vision and the wherewithal to carry it out. If your mission and your messages matter to your prospect, your communications should surround them with confidence.

Above all, ensure that your messages are consistent and clear and support your overall brand positioning. Make sure these include:

- Thank you.
- You can change the lives of others in a way that makes a difference for them and for you – and here's how.
- We appreciate you and your gift.
- We are a well-run organization.

- Our leadership is 100 percent invested; others also support our effort.
- I have given; please join me in making this difference.

Most campaigns will employ a wide variety of formal and informal communications tools to express these messages – everything from wallet-card talking points for solicitors to a regular newsletter, from direct mail to videos, from annual reports to web site updates, tours, media relations, events, speeches and more. Regardless:

- Begin with a communications plan, well-reasoned and supportive, not only of the campaign, but of your overall strategic plan and directions. Failure to plan is planning to fail.

- Focus on benefits and beneficiaries of the donor's investment – not features of the project. Few people want to fund a building; most would rather fund the ability to make a difference. The building simply is a means to that end.

- Integrate the look and feel of all materials, and make certain they are appropriate for the expectations of your audience.

- Communication is only part of the picture. Even the best messages and materials cannot replace solid fundraising and organizational fundamentals; they can only support them.

CASE FOR SUPPORT

At the core of all campaign communications is your Case for Support. It supports cultivation, solicitation, training and appreciation. In it resides the key messages of the campaign, easily culled for solicitations, presentations, grant requests, letters and the like.

The Case is part heart-tugger, part business plan. It is a brand extender, organizational overview, motivator and reinforcer. It is part confidence-builder and decision-justifier. It is a critical tool for solicitations and beyond.

A persuasive case stresses benefits throughout. It includes a brief introduction of the campaign and organization (history, mission, program and achievements), a clear description of the need and its impact on the community, and a convincing explanation of the solution, including campaign goal. Let it tell your story, and don't forget the call for action. Quotes and anecdotes from leaders – or better yet, those you serve – are powerful. Even more compelling: pictures of those who will benefit.

MONTHLY NEWSLETTER

This tool, informal and heartfelt, is a powerful, inexpensive means of maintaining momentum while communicating appreciation, news and progress to campaign leaders and donors. Some campaigns choose to distribute it monthly, others quarterly. Make certain it's the same day every publication (such as the first Monday of the month).

Delivered either online as a PDF or inline e-mail, or in a print version mailed (give recipients the choice), the monthly newsletter is written under the signature of the executive director or campaign chair. It typically starts with a compelling story, update or summary about the campaign's impact since last publication. It can include a campaign update and overview (total of gifts since last publication, progress toward goal, number of asks out, etc.), update on services delivered, mention of recent major gifts, volunteer highlight, news and updates, kudos, and a full listing of all new gifts and donors.

A simple layout and newsletter name work best. Keep the look and feel clean; the writing brief. Pictures are fine, but remember, they will eat up space and, depending on size, could keep some Internet servers from allowing them through (although you can compensate for this by embedding links to your server for the photos; ask your IT person for guidance).

CAMPAIGN VIDEO/DVD ONLINE

Many campaigns create a video or DVD version of the Case for Support that they use in quiet-phase one-on-one and small-group solicitations, as well as in larger gatherings during the public phase. If your campaign creates a quiet-phase donor and prospect page on your web site (password protected), add a streaming video link. Once you go public, move the link to the campaign-announcement section of your home page. Reference it in quiet cultivation and public-phase direct mail and other solicitations.

WALLET-CARD TALKING POINTS

From your Case for Support create three to five must-mention talking points about campaign scope, importance and benefits. Place these onto the front of a small card (size of a credit card) with your organization's mission statement or solicitation tips on the other side. Laminate them and distribute to all campaign volunteers. This will serve as a tool for training, a reminder before entering a cultivation or solicitation, and ready reference during solicitations.

END OF CAMPAIGN REVIEW

This is your time to shine, appreciate, thank and celebrate. Create a booklet – bound and in color if appropriate, copied and stapled if preferred. Include stories of campaign success, appreciation for and from campaign leaders, pictures from events, stories and thanks from beneficiaries (and perhaps even drawings or letters), progress update for construction or other outcomes of the campaign. Then include a list of every gift and every giver. In many ways, this is the same type of tool as your annual report. Send it to everyone who volunteered and all who gave. Include handwritten thank-you inscriptions in the front for volunteers and significant donors.

BEST PRACTICES

Send a campaign newsletter update every other month to current and former board members and trustees, donors, prospects and those interviewed for the project. It should feature recent campaign gifts, discuss progress and highlight a special volunteer.

Susan Schneweis
Hartsook Companies, Inc. (Lawrence, Kan.)

Network and listen every chance you get.

Paul Shuffield, Jr.
Southern Financial Partners (Arkadelphia, Ark.)

Create a 'Discover Week' series of special events, tours and groundbreakings that draws people to and culminates in public announcement of your capital campaign. It will engage supporters, generate press coverage and energize your staff.

Murray Blackwelder
Purdue University (West Lafayette, Ind.)

With capital campaigns, create a leadership committee outside of the typical campaign cabinet to identify bright people for cabinet and leadership roles. Set them apart and start the process. It especially works for organizations that don't have strong or experienced boards.

Jeanne Schmelzer, CFRE
Netzel Associates, Inc. (San Jose, Calif.)

We have started a thorough outcome evaluation of all our programs. We survey teachers, parents and participating students about benefits, behavioral changes and increased family communication on the covered issues. The Camp Fire agency is dedicated to developmental asset building through educational programs which teach self-reliance, responsibility, service, respect for self and others, as well as the prevention of child abuse and substance abuse.

Barbara VanHorn
Camp Fire USA New Jersey Council (Trenton, N.J.)

With the volume of e-mails we receive, and with viruses so rampant, those from people I don't know get pushed way back. It could be days before I read them – if I read them at all. Faxes, on the other hand, get seen immediately. I figure if someone takes time to write and send a fax, it must be important for them – and for me. I think faxes, regular mail and phone calls are becoming a lost art. Send me a fax every time!

Lee Ann Amerson
Fairbanks Community Mental Health Center (Fairbanks, Alaska)

Our Back to School with the Foundation campaign brought patrons and business into the schools for lunch and fundraising. We raised more than $100,000 for grants to teachers and schools.

Marcia Johnson
Springfield Public Schools (Springfield, Mo.)

We started an e-mail newsletter in December using a template designed by our webmaster. Once a month, he puts in graphics and pictures and sends it out. He figured out how to overcome the difficulty in sending such newsletters caused by some of the larger ISP platforms. It's been a tremendously well-received outreach by individuals and is working well.

Kristi Ericon, CFRE
Nevada Women's Fund (Reno, Nev.)

Build strong internal spirit by creating a positive, nurturing environment. Share goals, victories, insight, information and fun. Encourage involvement and ownership through regular communication, formal and, most important, informal.

Shelly Chinberg
Hartsook Companies, Inc. (Wichita, Kan.)

Develop a strong case statement for major gifts and capital campaigns.

Larry Rzepka
American Anthropological Association (Arlington, Va.)

Thank people, even if by mail, and ask them to call you.

Dave Targonski
Legion of Christ (Hamden, Conn.)

BEST PRACTICES FOR SUCCESSFUL SOLICITATIONS

Throw caution to the wind. Get out there and ask.
Jump into the breach and ask.

Jennifer Conroy
Canine Companions for Independence (Santa Rosa, Calif.)

*A billion here, a billion there, pretty soon
it adds up to real money.*

Senator Everett Dirksen
U. S. politician (1896-1969)

VALUE-ADDED SOLICITATIONS

No matter how you slice it, people give money to causes and organizations because, at some level, it makes them feel good. Something about giving causes them to experience a sense of satisfaction. That feeling of value, even of being valuable, may derive from different motivations. A few examples are donors:

- Being recognized as benefactors

- Being remembered positively after death

- Demonstrating financial stature

- Knowing people will benefit from their generosity

Most donors' giving is motivated by a combination plate of these and other motivations. The reason this is so important, particularly when dealing with the subject of solicitations, is because understanding that the donor has a strong need to feel valued will dispel any notion that fundraising is akin to begging.

Most development people already understand this, but in order to get volunteers and board members soliciting gifts effectively, it is usually necessary to retool their thinking about asking for major gifts.

The truth is, donors need to give – for their own personal reasons – as much or more than organizations need to receive. Soliciting a gift is not something to be undertaken with reticence or timidity. If you are informed and inspired by your organization's role in alleviating suffering, elevating the arts, nurturing children, battling a disease, or whatever your nonprofit is achieving in the world, then asking for money to support its mission is an awe-inspiring honor and responsibility.

Get this concept in your head and heart, impart this message to your volunteers and board members, solicit gifts from this vantage point and you will multiply the size and scope of the gifts you receive.

AMBIANCE AND "THE ASK"

Successful solicitations are often described as "asking the right person for the right amount of money at the right time." Let me add one more right ingredient – make your ask in the right place. It is better to schedule a solicitation appointment in a location that is free from distractions and interruptions.

Of course, the first rule of fundraising is that the donor is always right, so the right place to meet is always "wherever the donor wants to meet." However, it is best if you can avoid meeting for lunch at his club or at her office during work hours where there will be more commotion and interference.

Ideally, you want a place that is quiet, where you can ask the donor questions and listen carefully to the answers. You want a location where the donor is able to focus on what you have to say and feels free to ask any questions he or she might have.

Meeting in a busy restaurant may put you more at ease at first, but for the purpose of garnering a momentous gift, it is preferable to schedule your visit somewhere conducive to thoughtful and deliberate conversation.

THAT BEGS THE QUESTION ...

If you already know that several other donors have asked the same questions ("Why are you building something new instead of renovating the building you have?" "Why are you adding an ice rink to the recreation center when the city already has one?" "Who else is giving to this campaign?"), consider incorporating the answer into your next solicitation presentation. Keep learning and growing as you go. Have all solicitors make notes after every solicitation appointment to share so that you can perfect your game as you go along. Use the best practices in this book, keep refining your ask, and make every solicitation appointment better than the last.

Send a memo briefing for volunteers outlining strategies for gift solicitations that they can use during rehearsal.

Ginger Bower
YWCA of Metropolitan Washington (Washington, DC)

CHAPTER 9

KEEP IDENTIFYING NEW PROSPECT POOLS FOR SOLICITATION

WEALTH + INTEREST = MAJOR GIFTS

When was the last time your organization significantly expanded its list of prospective donors? What means do you use for locating new prospects and generating new gifts? Since it usually costs more in development dollars to generate a donor's first gift than to raise subsequent gifts from the same donor, organizations should do everything they can to identify likely donors. It may be easier to keep going back two and three times to the same wells and asking for repeat gifts, but it is absolutely essential to keep stretching out your sphere of influence. Never stop uncovering new prospect pools.

The two most effective criteria for identifying the donors most inclined to give major gifts to your organization are obvious: 1) wealth and 2) interest. Neither is sufficient without the other. Both need to be in place to secure successful solicitations.

One board of directors was inspired to stop serving "on a shoestring" and, instead, to raise major money for the nonprofit. The board members decided that the best way to get started was to purchase a lengthy (and expensive) mailing list of vastly wealthy individuals. The plan was to send a solicitation letter to each of the 10,000 richest people in the country and wait for the gifts to start rolling in to the office. They had the first component (wealth) in their sights, but without the second (interest) they would have paid thousands for a name and address list that would yield minimal returns. (Fortunately, they were talked out of this futile fundraising strategy.)

It is a philanthropic fact that to raise significant amounts of money, you need to talk to individuals who can give generous gifts – donors with great wealth – but being rich is not enough to make someone a likely donor. Donors have become increasingly more interested in giving to organizations that promote the same values they hold dear. "Making a difference" has evolved more into "making a difference in a specific way that matters to me."

That is why it is so important to find affluent donors who have a strong interest in your organization's mission. Otherwise, you will be expending your time and energy, as well as your organization's development dollars, pursuing donors who are not deeply moved by your message. They may think your organization is reputable, efficient and "doing good work" (in general), but unless they are like-minded and in step with your cause, you are unlikely to receive amounts equivalent to their capacity to give. Your job is to help them see how your organization upholds the values they hold dear.

To uncover new prospect pools, continue to ask board members and current donors to draw up a list of names –

wealthy friends, family and acquaintances who share their values and fall in line with your organization's core values. These individuals may not know about the nonprofit's work right now, but if they have shared values (the arts, education, the environment, etc.), then there is great potential for cultivating and increasing that interest.

WHO'S WHO?

While directories such as "Who's Who," "Standard & Poor's," and local business journals are still used by fundraisers to identify affluent individuals, the Internet has become an especially welcome tool for finding prospective pools. You can easily uncover detailed information about individuals' wealth and special interests. Nonprofits can now surf and search myriad sites for insider information. You can either hire a consulting firm or do it yourself, but remember, time is money and a nonprofit that manages its own research will still need to spend money to access the Web's most effective sites.

Lexis-Nexis and others will charge several hundred dollars a month to issue reports on demographics, stock holdings, real estate ownership, etc. The EDGARS report provides the salaries and other information about executives of publicly traded companies. Unless you know exactly what you are looking for, it may be more cost-effective to hire a professional.

No amount of research will give you a prospect's net worth, but knowing salary, real estate and stock holdings will allow you to approximate a number and combine that information with the past giving patterns and personal input from board members familiar with the prospect. At least this should help give you an asking number with the right amount of zeros following.

LEAVE NO STONE UNTURNED

Keep looking around your community for new leads to follow. Who are the major landowners? Who are the business owners? What major industries are located in your area? What are the interests of these industries' CEOs? Are there any second homes or vacation homes in your area? Do you know who lives in them? Are there any state or national celebrities who once called your town home? To what types of organizations and associations do people who care about your organization belong? Have you sat down with the bankers and financial consultants in your area to make sure they know about your organization and its mission? Have you considered every possible connection between your current constituents and new prospective pools? Once you have an idea that a prospective donor shares your organization's values, use today's technology and research tools to create a tailor-made plan for cultivation and solicitation.

Do your research. Key in on shared values. Get the gift.

BEST PRACTICES

About three years ago we formed a Financial Health Advisors Council (FHA) comprised of local accountants, attorneys, bank trust officers, financial advisors and others who advise their clients in planning for the distribution of their estates. Members of the group serve as advocates for our hospital system in the community and, when appropriate, help their clients include the hospital foundation in their estate plans. As a result of our relationship with FHA members, our planned gift commitments have increased dramatically.

Katharine Dennis
Scottsdale Healthcare Foundation (Scottsdale, Ariz.)

Our organization utilizes 25 vehicles that cumulatively log about 25,000 miles a week providing transportation to seniors. Recently we asked community leaders to 'sponsor a vehicle.' We put our organization's logo on the side, along with the sponsoring individual's personal or business name. It's a great way to let our community know about our organization and it makes those vehicles work just a little bit harder for us.

Megan Tarbert
Senior Solutions (Anderson, S.C.)

Every year or so we have luncheons for the major attorneys, trust officers and accountants in town – a separate function for each firm. Our president and foundation executive director update them on College and Foundation happenings. One person in each firm is our contact person to help set up the event. That person is the contact when we follow up and deliver our College/Foundation Annual Reports. We ask these contacts to place the annual reports in the reception areas for their clients in hopes that discussions about tax savings, estate planning and charitable gifts include us.

Harry I. Harelik
The McLennan Community College Foundation (Waco, Tex.)

Not forgetting our employees are also donors and wish to contribute to our mission, in April we will run our annual employee campaign, 'The Power of Potential,' through payroll deduction contributions. A $4 per month median gift leads to $100,000 in annual pledges.

Michele Crane
The Bethphage Foundation (Omaha, Neb.)

The National Kidney Foundation of the Virginias identified a prospect that was a vendor to the organization's Kidney Cars program. As a result, the vendor was solicited and pledged $100,000 to the research endowment.

Wendy D. Doyle
Hartsook Companies, Inc. (Kansas City, Mo.)

We are community driven. Everything from grants to solicitations begins with local stakeholder ideas.

Mary Harding
Nebraska Environmental Trust (Lincoln, Neb.)

We have more than 400,000 members. We challenged each one to donate $1 as a fundraiser and also to build our donor base.

Chad Sorce
Young American Bowling Alliance (Greendale, Wisc.)

We use the Web to look up addresses of senior retirement communities. We then run our donor database by address and find donors who live in those buildings. We then talk to those donors about coming to the building and doing an introduction to Girl Scouts.

Patricia Broughton
Girl Scouts of Chicago (Chicago, Ill.)

We send out action alerts to our members via broadcast e-mail regarding advocacy action at the state level. This is a member service that helps people think of us, so when we ask for money, they'll feel good.

Brad Collins, CFRE
American Solar Energy Society (Boulder, Colo.)

During campaign assessment or prospect identification, it is critical to garner candid feedback from all Board members. Be inclusive, not selective. This not only allows you to gather insight from those leaders closest to your organization, but helps secure their involvement and commitment early in the process.

Jennifer Aday
Hartsook Companies, Inc. (Kansas City, Mo.)

We are a private elementary school and realize our future lies in our alumni and their support. This needs to begin early and be consistent to create a culture of giving that remains throughout their adult years. For them, we have created a Dollar-a-Year Club in place of an annual-giving program. It starts when they are freshmen in high school. For each year they have been gone from us, they donate a dollar. For example, a high school freshman's contribution is $1, but a high school senior contributes $4. A sophomore in college sends $6, and so on. These young donors feel invested in "their school" and are proud to find their names in our annual stewardship magazine, The Spirit.

Kathryn B. Knox, ACFRE
The Independence School (Newark, Del.)

CHAPTER 10
PRE-SOLICITATION PREPARATION

WHAT DO WE KNOW FOR SURE?

Even if you have assembled an impressive list of affluent and interested prospects, there are still more housekeeping items to tick off before heading out to solicit a gift. As Arlene Snyder reminds us: It's "ready, aim, fire!" and not "ready, fire, aim."

Nail down the presolicitation basics before setting up any donor meetings to ask for money. Evaluate each donor file. Do we know:

- Everything we should about this donor?
- What organizations he/she has given to in the past?
- What aspect of our organization he/she cares about most?
- What current donors are acquaintances of this prospect?
- What are his/her interests, values and concerns?
- If he/she would be interested in a naming opportunity?

- What naming opportunities and amounts we can suggest?

- If sufficient cultivation has occurred to make a solicitation?

- A specific, realistic, but generous gift amount for the ask?

- Who would be the best person to ask this donor for a gift?

- Who would be the best complement to go with the solicitor?

- If our campaign materials state our case in a clear and convincing way?

- If all solicitors have been thoroughly trained to solicit a gift?

- If solicitors have made a gift in an amount equal to or more than the individual they are soliciting (whenever possible)?

- That 100 percent of our board has already given?

- That our organization has a clean record of good stewardship?

Going through this or a similar list of questions will give your team assurance that this is the right time to solicit a gift from a particular donor, or it will uncover holes in your presolicitation strategies.

MATCH UP SOLICITORS FINANCIALLY AND PHILOSOPHICALLY

There are plenty of development directors who are extremely successful at asking for major gifts. However, the ideal scenario is to have a development director who knows how to draw out the very best solicitations from board members and volunteers – especially those who already have a strong relationship with prospects.

It is best when a solicitor already has an established connection with the prospect either socially or through business or some other commonality and is considered a financial peer. Try to find as many connections as possible – attended the same school, belong to the same organization, etc.

Ensure that solicitors have already made their gifts so that they can answer honestly and enthusiastically when asked, "Are you personally supportive of this campaign?" Give solicitors plenty of time to absorb the case and use role playing to ask and answer any anticipated questions that may arise during a solicitation. The more prepared a solicitor feels, the more confidence she will exude, and the more convincing she will be in her solicitation.

If you have already committed proper donor research and cultivation to the cause, then the question should not be whether your organization will receive a gift, but how much it will receive.

DON'T FORGET TO EQUIP SOLICITORS ADEQUATELY

As fundraisers, we talk a lot about knowing our donors, but when it comes to successful solicitations, it is just as important to know the strengths and weaknesses of your solicitors before going into a donor meeting.

One generous board member, who had actually given the lead gift toward a campaign, was chosen to ask an acquaintance for a $500,000 gift. Adequate cultivation had already taken place. It was clear that the prospect cared about and respected the organization. Everything was pointing to a successful and financially lucrative evening.

The board member and development director arrived on time and the prospective donor was the perfect host, offering a seat, a drink and congenial conversation. The development director was thrilled. He knew that everyone there understood the purpose of the meeting – asking the donor for money. His role for this meeting was to serve as an extra set of eyes and ears, to answer questions, and to give moral support as the board member asked for his first gift ever. "It must be about time," the development director thought to himself. "He's going to ask here in a minute." Another 10 minutes went by. "He must be getting ready to launch in anytime now!" The board member continued to chat amiably. Another 10 minutes ticked by slowly – agonizingly slowly.

Even the host was obviously ready to get things moving along. He reached into his coat pocket, pulled out his checkbook and announced, "Well, we all know why you're here. Let me go ahead and give you my gift for this campaign." He slid the $10,000 check across the table and the board member, relieved, picked it up and thanked him for his gift.

What happened there? The board member left a lot of money on the table. If he had asked for $500,000, there is no guarantee that he would have gotten it all, but the gift would surely have been closer to the mark than the one they received.

Training solicitors to know what to expect, to be prepared to answer questions about the campaign, to ask for a specific gift within the first few minutes of a donor meeting, and other solicitation basics will make the difference between a wildly successful campaign and one that just ticks along slowly – agonizingly slowly.

BEST PRACTICES

We are inviting our 50 top major-gift prospects to a teleconference call with our program director on human rights to hear about his recent visit to Bangkok Conference on rights for 'sweatshop' workers. This is the first of a series of planned conference calls.

Catherine Onyemelukwe
(New York, N.Y.)

It is critical that Board members solicit other Board members. Professional development staff must fight the urge to circumvent the process and handle those 'asks' themselves. For one thing, it's easier to say no to a staff member, or to offer a gift of lesser value. But also, until a Board member hears the heartfelt reasons a peer has given, they will not gain true appreciation for the gift and the importance of giving to their capacity. This also means ensuring enough time for all Board-to-Board solicitations to occur without rush. Start early.

Kathie Riggs
Montana State University-Billings (Billings, Mont.)

Extensive follow-up and training courses.

Rajeev Dua
South Asian Fund Raising Group (New Delhi, India)

As the first fundraiser for an organization with a reluctant board, I pledged a percentage of my salary to the annual fund at my introductory board meeting, while at the same time asking for board support and cooperation.

Greg Tjapkes
Hina Makua (Kanohe, Hawaii)

When preparing for meetings or phone calls with potential supporters whom I do not know, I first research their interests on the Internet or ask others about them. I look for something or someone we have in common. I mark this information on a note card and reread it just before our conversation. This little bit of insight allows me to break the ice and quickly overcome those initial jitters.

Elaine Fox
North Valley Jewish Community Center (Los Angeles, Calif.)

When going through lists of names in search of prospects with volunteers or other staff, start at the end of the list and work backward. People in the second half of the alphabet or at the end of the list often get less attention than the top of the list or the first half of the alphabet.

Robert F. Hartsook, JD, EdD
Hartsook Companies, Inc. (Wrightsville Beach, N.C.)

Plan. Remember. It's 'ready, aim, fire!' not 'ready, fire, aim.'

Arlene Snyder, CFRE
Western Pennsylvania Allegheny Hospital Foundation
(Pittsburgh, Pa.)

Outline discussions, save document copies, archive and keep information.

Chris Walker
Inner Form (Lancaster, Pa.)

I had my volunteers communicate via e-mail with each other, then they forwarded me the whole chain. That gives me good information about their interests and philosophy. And when the donor hears from me, they begin to see me on the same level as the board members.

Yezdyar Kaoosji
Friends of the Indian School (Los Angeles, Calif.)

Data management is an integral part of the process to convert prospects to donors and donors to major supporters. Set policies for data management and step-by-step procedures to ensure information entered is consistent, accurate, logical and extractable. Inaccurate and incomplete data that is perceived to be accurate can be more harmful than no data at all.

Judy Turner
Hartsook Companies, Inc. (Kansas City, Mo.)

We're increasing professionalism through a one-year mentoring program. We pair experienced and inexperienced fundraisers when they sign up as newcomers for our AFP chapter. We have many mentors for our nonprofits.

Janet Carter
Boys & Girls Club of Saline County (Benton, Ark.)

The first step in developing a strategy for a prospective donor should be comprehensive donor research. That will help make your next steps clearer and more productive.

Leslie Linzy
Hartsook Companies, Inc. (Kansas City, Mo.)

Give Trustees a clear focus for cultivation and solicitation. Ask them to help you solicit one company and two individuals for support. That's all. Ten is too many, and even five bogs the Trustee down. Just focus them on three prospects and give them the background they need to set up the meeting, then go with them on the appointments so they don't worry about what to say. Help them along. You succeed, and they do, too!

John R. Mitterling
North Carolina Symphony (Raleigh, N.C.)

CHAPTER 11
THE MOST PRODUCTIVE FORM OF FUNDRAISING

Trust me. Face-to-face solicitations with affluent, interested, cultivated donors are the very best means for raising money for your organization. Everything else – auctions, phone-a-thons, direct mail, grants, web-based fundraising, special events, etc. – may generate money, but compared to personal solicitations that ask the right person at the right time for the right amount of money, they are "also-rans."

Make major-gift solicitations your bread-and-butter fundraising strategy. You can add the preserves later.

LOOK ON (AND SOLICIT FROM) THE BRIGHT SIDE

Enter every solicitation with the most positive outlook and case for support possible. Donors like to reward success and advance good ideas. They do not like to be asked to help organizations out of financial straits. Even if your nonprofit is in a tight place, it is probably better, for solicitation purposes, to keep accentuating the positive.

For example, one organization was tight on space and in desperate need of a new facility for the education component of their mission. They took out a loan for a building and used some of their savings to renovate the facility. A year later they recognized their need to undertake a capital campaign – their very first one. They started the campaign (without the benefit of professional counsel) by making a list of everything they needed – capital improvements, program money, operating expenses, and their greatest wish list item – debt reduction. It did not take them long to realize that they were in way over their heads.

After speaking with a fundraising consultant and undergoing a thorough campaign assessment, the organization learned that prospective donors were not as excited about paying off the note as they were. Donors wanted to be part of something that was moving forward. Armed with this new insight, the organization revamped its campaign to showcase the elements that excited and inspired donors.

While they had to set aside paying off their debt until later, the campaign helped them acquire so many new donors and re-energize existing donors in such a way that giving was increased across the board – not just the capital campaign, but annual gifts as well. Even though they still had to pay down the note through installments, the end was in sight and debt reduction was no longer the center of their universe.

Never ignore or gloss over your organization's deficits or shortcomings, but also never highlight them to raise money. Legitimate needs are sellable, but self-inflicted wounds are not. "We really need your money to keep the lights on ... pay salaries ... keep gas in the buses, etc." This is not an inspiring message.

Before walking in the door of a solicitation, silence any nay saying thoughts and prepare to deliver a message that says, "We are an organization with a great cause that affects lives in great ways and we will use your money to achieve great things!"

Always solicit from the right side of the issues. Always solicit from the bright side of your organization's mission.

DONOR-FOCUSED SOLICITATIONS

Unless they are careful, enthusiastic fundraisers can end up spending too much time during solicitations talking about what the organization does and too little time listening to what the donor wants to support. There is a tendency to think that you are "winning" if you are allowed to make your whole presentation without interruption. "The donor's listening, so I must be doing well." Wrong. You "win" when the donor is speaking and you are listening. You are winning because you are learning what the donor cares about, what he or she wants to discuss.

Donors understand that you are there to solicit a gift. The question is, how big a gift will you get? Going on and on about a particular aspect of the campaign (one that is most exciting to you) may make you animated and interesting to listen to, but it will not get you more money unless the donor cares about the subject as much as you do.

Rather than talking on and on about the various components of the campaign, stop and ask relevant questions. The donor should have received a case for support at least a week earlier. The case should have laid out the need, the solution, and the fact that money is being raised to achieve a goal. Rather than elaborating on what you think is important, ask the donor, "What did you see as the most compelling need in this campaign?" The answer may surprise you. "I want to see more done with scholarships" or "I really think it's important to get a good endowment going."

By the way, there is a myth that endowment money is harder to raise than money for bricks and mortar. Does this not reflect more on fundraisers than on donors? In other words, maybe it is harder for fundraisers to speak convincingly and passionately about endowment than it is for them to describe and illustrate a new building. Most major donors are also good businesspersons and understand the fiscal wisdom of establishing large endowments. If the donor cares about endowment, key in on that aspect of the campaign and use your time together more effectively.

Solicitations need to be more donor-focused and less organization-centered. Let donors tell you what they want to support. A listening fundraiser is a winning solicitor.

When Silence is Golden

Solicitors should enter a donor meeting with a short letter in hand that verifies the amount of the ask. While there are several good reasons for this, one of the benefits is that the ask amount should be based on hard facts and nonemotional decision making. Once a person is sitting face-to-face with a donor (especially if there is any lack of confidence on the part of the solicitor), he or she might be tempted to dial down the amount of the ask. Putting the number in black and white keeps the solicitation on track.

The letter, presented after the verbal ask has been made, should simply convey the organization's esteem and appreciation for the donor's time and any previous gifts and ask for a specific gift amount. This step also helps avoid miscommunication. "He sent $16,000! But he agreed to

$60,000!" You can never rectify a mistake like that. Can you imagine? "Excuse me, Mr. Jones. You heard me wrong. I said $60,000. Would you please send us the remaining $44,000? Thanks. Ba-bye."

Once you ask for the gift, "Mr. Jones, would you please consider making a gift of $60,000?" and hand Mr. Jones the short letter of intent, it is time to play the children's schoolyard game Statue. Statues come in many shapes and sizes, but they have at least two things in common: 1) they are still and 2) they are silent. Once you have asked for the gift, everything is officially out of your hands. The ball is, as they say, in the donor's court. Do not add two more important points. Do not comment on the lovely topiary in the corner of the room. Do not ask about his wife's lumbago. Just make like a statue – still and silent.

GIVE DONORS SOME ELBOW ROOM

Many donors, especially business owners and entrepreneurs, appreciate flexibility in the details of their giving arrangements. One donor made it clear during times of cultivation that he really wanted to become a million-dollar giver. There was something about that benchmark that had value to him. He mentioned it in passing and the fundraiser, being a savvy sort, tucked the information away for future use.

When a campaign presented an appropriate time to ask the donor for a major gift, the fundraiser was ready. "Would you please consider giving a million dollars to this organization?" Even though the donor had mentioned "one million" over coffee six months earlier, he actually hesitated when asked. A downturn in the economy had slightly tarnished his hopes of reaching the million-dollar mark. The fundraiser waited for a response (still and silent, I might add) until finally the donor spoke. "I really want to do this, but I just don't know if it's possible the way things are right now."

The clever and creative fundraiser was prepared. "What about giving the gift over a five-year period, but without giving 20 percent each and every year? Give this amount now and as circumstances change you can make larger installments down the road." Since the donor/business owner had lived through a number of these economic cycles, he was confident that over five years he would be able to complete his gift. It took only four and a half years for the donor to finish his pledge. However, the satisfaction of achieving his life-long goal of being a million-dollar giver began the night he said "yes" to the well-conceived ask.

TAKE YES FOR AN ANSWER

If there has been proper donor research and cultivation prior to a solicitation, fundraisers should expect to hear "Yes!"

- Yes. I will give the asked-for amount.
- Yes. I will give an amount less than what you have asked.
- Yes. I am supportive of your organization, but I cannot give and this is why …

If a donor gives an unqualified "No," then the organization's research and cultivation process needs to be put under a microscope, diagnosed and treated immediately. CODE RED. STAT!

Face-to-face donor solicitations should be the most exciting, most anticipated event of a fundraiser's occupational life. It is the culmination of hard work and good instincts, and, all in all, the hardest part will probably be waiting – like a statue – for the donor's response.

BEST PRACTICES

One person's dime is another person's dollar. Treat each and every donor to your cause with the utmost respect. Doing so will undoubtedly come back to you, tenfold.

Laurie Ward, MS
Hartsook Companies, Inc. (Minneapolis, Minn.)

We tell volunteer fundraisers to keep a smile on their face, that it's okay to ask for money. Fundraising is not a bad word. If a volunteer doesn't like to ask, tell them you'll put them somewhere else so they don't have to ask. We had a lawyer who said, 'You don't want me asking anybody for money. I've lived in this town all my life. I've probably sued everybody at least once!' We found something else for him to do.

Carole Wright, CFRE
Resurrection Catholic Missions (Montgomery, Ala.)

When soliciting a gift, don't be afraid to ask for more money than is in your "comfort zone." If the right person is asking at the right time for the right project, you will be successful. The best-case scenario is you'll get the gift; the worst is that the prospect will be flattered you thought they could give such a high amount!

Anne E. Johnson, MEd
Hartsook Companies, Inc. (Kansas City, Mo.)

Featuring an expert on planned giving, we use technology to sponsor and present tax and estate planning information to attorneys, bankers and other financial planners. Interactive satellite and web-based seminars are an effective means to reach multiple locations, increasing reach and efficiency. At the same time the expert is providing value to the participants, those participants (many of whom have access to trusts and estates) connect in a positive way with our organization.

Robb Waugus
The Salvation Army of the Fox Cities (Appleton, Wisc.)

Be transparent and honest with donors, volunteers and partners.

Unsigned

Each appointment with a donor has a purpose. An ask is always made.

Sandra Hea
World Vision Canada (Mississauga, Ontario)

Use every tool available when preparing a strategic solicitation plan. Oftentimes, critical points of view and nuances of the donor are not sought from those volunteers who know the prospect best. Do not rush the solicitation. It will result in a less than favorable outcome.

Chad Linzy
Hartsook Companies, Inc. (Kansas City, Mo.)

Transition capital donors to annual donors.

Mark Trujillo, CFRE
Greater Phoenix Economic Council (Scottsdale, Ariz.)

Whenever possible, include a banker, stockbroker or estate planning attorney on your development committee (or whatever committee is doing confidential prospect evaluations). When discussing ranges of giving capability and recommended requests, many times they will indicate if the request should be higher, lower or is on target.

Mandy Pons
Hartsook Companies, Inc. (Albuquerque, N.M.)

CHAPTER 12
VARIATIONS ON A THEME

In the same way that fundraisers should leave no stone unturned in prospecting for new donors, it is wise to use every fundraising strategy available to your organization – as long as you give face-to-face solicitations with affluent interested donors the bulk of your time and attention. Here is a laundry list of some basic fundraising strategies employed by organizations:

- Direct mail
- Phone-a-thons
- Web-based fundraising
- Grants
- Special events
- Silent auctions

DIRECT MAIL

Mail appeals take somewhat of a shotgun approach. Your message is scattered abroad in the hope of reaching a target. Organizations can either purchase mailing lists or compile their own using in-house data such as alumni lists. Conventional wisdom says to expect a single-digit response somewhere around 1 to 3 percent. (And that is if your mailing list is not entirely cold to your cause.)

Never use direct mail to ask for large gifts. Its only purpose is for mass communication. If this strategy is used during a campaign, make sure you have exhausted all prospects for face-to-face solicitations before going to a public or mass-ask. You can generally assume the less personal the ask, the smaller the gift.

PHONE-A-THONS

When it comes to being the brunt of derisive jokes, tele-marketers have joined the infamous ranks of lawyers and politicians. They have become fair game. People have never loved the interruption, but now they are beginning to view phone solicitations as they do Internet spam – unwelcome and intrusive.

Yet, there is still a place for phone-a-thons in the public phase of a campaign. It remains an effective means for upgrading modest donors to a higher level of giving or reinitiating past donors who have dropped off over the last year or so. For a community-wide campaign, it can work to call and announce, "Perhaps you've seen our sign at First and Main. Our campaign is just about to reach its goal. Would you like to be part of that last push to the top?" Used judiciously, a phone-a-thon is still an inexpensive and potentially effective means for public fundraising.

WEB-BASED FUNDRAISING

Not only is the Internet a gold mine for gaining donor insights and gathering grant information, but there are some other practical ways to use the Web to catch cash for your organization.

If your nonprofit is part of a national affiliate, make sure Internet users can easily link to your home page via the national organization. It is a good idea to have someone in your office periodically search your web site just as a first-time viewer would. Web designers and even those who update the information on your site may not be aware of small annoyances unless they start from scratch and search through as a novice.

For example, it is surprising how many organizations fail to place contact information on the home page. Put all the basics – phone with area code, fax, e-mail and street address with city, state and zip – right up there where people can see it. Why should a viewer have to click to "contact us" when all they need is a phone number?

Is there a prominent icon on the home page for anyone wanting to volunteer their time and money? Make it easy for them. Have you Googled your organization's name or general information to determine if people can find you quickly? If you have gone to all the time and expense of setting up a web site, make sure you are getting the most clicks for your cash. Take note of the pluses and minuses of other organization's web sites and embrace those best practices as your own.

SILENT AUCTIONS AND SPECIAL EVENTS

Silent auctions and special events are as much a method for raising your organization's visibility among new and prospective donors as a means for raising money. Use these activities to promote the nonprofit's mission and personality. These events come with a price tag, so make sure they become signature events. Especially when used as an annual occasion (scheduled for the same month every year), an event will build interest over time. Donors will begin marking their calendars in advance and plan ahead for giving opportunities.

One university holds a silent auction of donated quilts the same time every year. Many donors, particularly parents and grandparents, wait for this fall event to purchase large, expensive quilts for upcoming weddings. The tradition and consistency in theme and timing of this event ensures that there will always be donors/buyers waiting to contribute to the school while they meet an important need of their own. The development office does not have to worry whether people will participate in this special event. They know donors are actually anticipating it and looking forward to the holiday kickoff.

THE GOAL IS GAINING GREAT GIFTS FOR YOUR ORGANIZATION

Clearly, there are many ways to raise money for your organization. The most effective and productive means is to secure donors who know what you do, personally care about your cause and have the ability to support it financially with big gifts. However, the goal is always to get gifts from your donors and into your nonprofit's coffers. Whatever ethical means you use – special events or silent auctions, telemarketing or web-based technology – just make sure your methods reflect well on your organization and reap the results you deserve and desire.

BEST PRACTICES

We are a small religious organization. We needed a wheelchair van for retired Sisters. We did a one-time direct mail (Wheel Appeal Campaign). In three months we raised more than $60,000. Target your audience. It worked!

Jeanette Fettig, CSC
Sisters of the Holy Cross (Notre Dame, Ind.)

When grant writing, follow the instructions! Make sure your proposal budget is accurate. If you need more room, play with your margins or most forms are available online. Employ succinct, tight writing.

Kathy Rogers, CFRE
Grantwriter (Golden Eagle, Ill.)

When drafting grant requests, type the headings of the narrative section first. Under each heading, type, in italics, the information from the 'criteria section,' which tells you what the reviewers seek. This helps you address the questions fully. It also helps when you are asking other members of your staff for input. Once your final draft is ready, simply delete the italicized section and you are ready to send.

Jean Kresse
Hartsook Companies, Inc. (Des Moines, Iowa)

We hire, train and highly empower a very small group of students to conduct a phone-a-thon. They generate the same volume as 20 volunteers. It's a paid position with incentive-based pay – true telemarketing. We give them considerable autonomy so they can fit their work schedule around school and other activities. Last fall we enjoyed a 35 percent increase in phone-a-thon revenue, and we're hoping to cross the 50 percent threshold this spring.

Michael Mason
Maryville University (St. Louis, Mo.)

Make your event more than a fundraiser, make it a party – make it the 'have-to-be-there' event. How? Make it a FUNraiser. Give your guests reasons why they should give up their time and why they would want to come and be involved.

Diane Creed
American Diabetes Association (Southbury, Conn.)

Meeting deadlines is critical for grant submissions and for ongoing communication with grant makers. To ensure I manage the process, I post the various projects' deadlines on a wall calendar. Each notation prompts me to stay on track. It is a very effective, yet simple system.

Mary Stuart, MPH
St. Francis Hospital and Medical Center (Hartford, Conn.)

Customize renewal mailings to your donor levels, segmented into categories such as $1 to $100, $101 to $250 and so on up to $1,000. While keeping the case statement elements consistent, provide a more in-depth and informative letter as you move up the categories. In all letters, remind the donor of the size of their previous gift, thank them for it, and then ask for a larger gift. A phone call or a personal visit asking for the gift is most effective if the universe of $1,000-plus donors is manageable. Otherwise, an even more in-depth and personalized letter would be appropriate.

John Marshall, CFRE
The Salvation Army of Greater New York (New York, N.Y.)

Silent auctions should consist of no more than 100 to 125 packaged items. They should be organized according to categories with fun, descriptive category names. The packages should have values of no less than $100 and opening bids should be no more than 30 percent of the retail value.

Laverne Pitts
Corvallis Public Schools Foundation (Corvallis, Ore.)

Follow up through telemarketing. It gives the opportunity for two-way conversation, to answer concerns and to explain the 'whys' of what we do.

Mickey Nickelson
Archdiocese of St. Paul/Minneapolis (St. Paul, Minn.)

Always include a No. 9 return envelope (3 by 8 inches) with your direct-mail appeals, not the smaller envelopes you sometimes see. The bigger the envelope, the bigger the check! The No. 9 fits just inside the standard No. 10 envelope you would use for the initial mailing. But remember: A big envelope sent with a poorly crafted solicitation is not as effective as a smaller envelope sent with a thoughtful letter.

Vicki Ronald
Benton County Sunshine School (Bentonville, Ark.)

Insert a response card (either postage paid or with a postage-paid envelope) in all publications. This card will include a check box offering more information about the publication's topic. Add check boxes for requesting information not related to the publication's topic. This is especially effective for introducing planned-giving options. Mark each card with a unique code so you can track its source and the response.

Dan Chegwidden, CFP
Michigan State University (East Lansing, Mich.)

Facilitate pledge payments by using coupon books and pre-addressed mailing labels. It saves time, postage and paper.

Rev. Carl Pieber
Diocese of Galveston-Houston (Houston, Tex.)

BEST PRACTICES FOR SHOWING RECOGNITION & APPREICATION

Where should the development director stand in the photo with a donor? Immediately to the right of the photographer. It's not about YOU – it's about THEM!

Mary Wuller
Visitation Academy (St. Louis, Mo.)

*The best way to have a good idea
is to have a lot of ideas.*

Dr. Linus Pauling
Nobel Prize winner (1901-1994)

VALUE YOUR DONORS

Forty years ago there were approximately 25,000 nonprofit organizations in the United States. One of the last figures posted – though no one can keep an exact count – is more than two million! More 501(c)3's are formed every day. Obviously, this presents a fundraising challenge. At the same time, it is a good motivator for all nonprofits to rethink their fundraising efforts, especially when it comes to showing appreciation and giving donors the recognition they deserve.

Donors have many choices. Organizations cannot risk taking any donor for granted. We all know that it is more difficult and costly to secure a first-time donor than to maintain the ones you already have. Therefore, it is even more important that an organization's systems and procedures for showing appreciation and recognition are at their best. Retaining donors is a must. Never let a donor feel unappreciated or undervalued.

UPGRADING GIFTS

Does your organization use designated levels to recognize tiers of gift giving – Benefactors (more than $10,000), Regents (more than $5,000), etc.? Keep providing new ceilings of giving and new benefits for upgrading to the next level. Just as airlines will ask if a passenger would like to upgrade a seat for an extra amount of money, give donors a good reason to up their gifts. If the seats at the back of the plane were as comfortable as the ones in first class, why would anyone care to move up? Make sure the demarcations are distinct and that each tier is significantly more desirable than the one before.

When was the last time you asked a Regent if he or she would like to join the austere ranks of the Benefactors club (with all the accompanying benefits)? Are any of your Benefactors ready to move up to the next level of giving? Keep the brass ring within their grasp. Keep inventing new ways to make giving to your organization the best game in town.

Barring some unforeseen economic turn or personal crisis, donors should be increasing their gifts every year. However, this will only happen when donors feel that their gifts are appreciated and that they are receiving the proper recognition for their philanthropy. Not all donors want the same level of recognition or reward for their philanthropy, but whatever their hopes or expectations, make sure you meet and surpass their highest aspirations.

Packaging is important to help position your institution. At Purdue University we packaged: $56 million in gift announcements, four dedications, and three ground breakings – all in all more than 30 different events that ended with Homecoming. This all happened within a 10-day period. The results were much higher news coverage and a great sense of momentum – two great results! You can do it at your institution, too!

Murray Blackwelder, MPA
Purdue University (West Lafayette, Ind.)

CHAPTER 13

RECOGNITION & APPRECIATION – DONORS DESERVE BOTH

SIMILAR, BUT NOT SYNONYMOUS

Donors give gifts for a multitude of reasons. Despite their wide and varied motivations for giving, all donors deserve to be recognized and appreciated for their generosity.

Sometimes you will see "recognition" and "appreciation" used almost interchangeably. Although they are similar, they are not synonymous. Recognition and appreciation can be simply contrasted in this way:

- Appreciation demonstrates – to the donor – the value of his or her gift.
- Recognition demonstrates – publicly, to others – the value of the donor's gift.

Donors deserve both.

SHOW AND TELL

What is the best way to show appreciation to and recognize a major donor? That's easy. Whatever is most meaningful to the donor. Did I just hear you say, "Thanks a lot, Bob!"? Well, give me a minute and I will explain – but first, an illustration.

In the movie "Return to Me" with David Duchovny and Minnie Driver, a wealthy philanthropist has given a "sizeable donation" to build a new gorilla habitat. He approaches several people at a fundraising event and asks if they have heard about his sizeable donation and then in hushed tones adds, "Strictly anonymous, of course."

In reality, this humorous and unlikely scenario is not so funny when the wrong methods of recognition are used on the wrong donors. Some donors insist on anonymity. Others seek widespread recognition. What honors and excites one donor may offend or, at least, be less than inspiring to another. Just as good donor research allowed you to understand the best means for soliciting a gift, "knowing your donor" means understanding and respecting the way each one wants to be recognized.

As difficult a task as it may be, it is important for a development office to have a good idea what their major donors find meaningful. As often as possible, write down their preferences. Do you have policies and procedures in place for donors who want their gifts to remain anonymous? Unless you do, it is easy for an unwitting breach of confidentiality to occur. Most donors will want to be recognized among their peers as having been generous and influentially connected with the organization they support, but for those for whom anonymity is a moral or personal decision, you must make this sacrosanct.

THANK YOU. THANK YOU. THANK YOU.

The true test of appreciation is that it hits the mark; it makes a donor feel that the organization is genuinely thankful for the gift and that they highly esteem the donor as a benefactor.

Appreciation can be demonstrated in many ways – through methods that are lavish, effusive, elaborate and expensive or means that are subtle, understated, clear and simple. One is not necessarily better than another, except as it reflects authentic appreciation.

The best way to ensure that your organization conveys meaningful appreciation that hits the mark is to be an organization that: 1) genuinely and unceasingly is grateful to donors for their support, and 2) expresses thankfulness in ways that make an emotional connection.

The difference is not in the size or grandeur of the act, but in the sincerity of the action. Donors can recognize whether a "thank you" is a cut-and-paste job or a heartfelt expression uniquely tailored to fit.

Whether you are writing a note of thanks or picking up the phone to make a donor call, stop – if only for a few seconds – and think about what the gift means to the individuals you serve. Write from this place of gratitude, not simply from the desk of a happy development director who has worked hard to raise money, but from the pathos of one who understands the difference the gift has made in the lives of others. Write from a heart of humility and authentic thankfulness. Make your call (write your letter, deliver your speech, order the plaque, etc.) with an awareness of the impact this gift has made, and you will dramatically increase your ability to connect with the donor. Making that connection will greatly increase your ability to raise money from this donor in the future.

"YOU HAVE MADE A DIFFERENCE"

There are so many ways to show appreciation and recognition – from notes to naming opportunities, from mugs to memorials, and everything in between. The most important thing is to understand the need to show authentic appreciation and to give donors the recognition they deserve. Donors who feel that their gifts are not taken for granted are more likely to continue and probably increase their giving. Not only that, but donors who experience this kind of heartfelt treatment, even after years of giving, are more likely to consider a bequest.

Appreciation says, "We are grateful for your gift. It really made a difference." Recognition says, "We want others to know how respected and admired you are as a benefactor. You really made a difference."

By conveying private gestures of gratitude and showing public displays of donor recognition, an organization can transform regular donors into major donors and major gifts into planned gifts.

Never underestimate the power of saying "thank you" and meaning it.

BEST PRACTICES

As part of our Leadership Giving Society (we define leadership gifts as those between $1,000 and $10,000), we have instituted the '10-Percent Club.' Members enter an open-ended commitment to increase their pledge by 10 percent each year. Those who join this Club receive special notice in our Leadership Giving Society publication, as well as a special thank-you gift card and other recognition.

Mary Clark
Capital Area United Way (Lansing, Mich.)

Pay attention to your planned giving donors, and don't ignore them once they have pledged their gift. The relationship begins – not ends – when they make the gift. They expect a lifetime partnership. Make them a part of all you are doing. Get them involved and build a sense of ownership. They've already bought in. Keep them informed. They are partners. Don't forget them.

Rebecca Zimmer, CFRE
National Benevolent Association (St. Louis, Mo.)

Thank You! Thank You! Thank You! You can never say it enough.

Mickey Alvino
Deborah Hospital Foundation (Bayside, N.Y.)

We have received more than 4,000 automobiles as donations. I call every donor personally to say thank you.

Lee Schaefer
Volunteers of America (Cincinnati, Ohio)

We respond with a handwritten note to any comments donors make with their gift or response to solicitation. Example: A new $15 donor wrote a note to a response piece that said, 'It's not much, but it helps. I'm 90 and living in a (nursing) home.' I wrote him back a nice note thanking him – and now I'm going to visit him to talk about a bequest.

Patti Holmes, CFRE
FamilyLinks (Pittsburgh, Pa.)

For every gift we receive, or every group presentation we make, we prepare a certificate of appreciation on parchment-like paper. We print it in-house, and mount it in a Plexiglass frame. We then call the donor or organization head to set up another visit so we can present the certificate (which gives us one more point of contact for cultivation and relationship building). Even our major donors truly appreciate this simple expression of our gratitude. We often see the certificates on walls and the presentation mentioned in newsletters – yet another chance for our organization's name to be seen.

Sharon Akers
United Cerebral Palsy of Central Maryland (Baltimore, Md.)

Personally letting people know their gifts are appreciated brings positive results. Several years ago The Salvation Army of Kansas City set a goal during the Christmas campaign to call and thank every donor making a gift of $500 or more within 24 hours of receiving the gift. The first year they called 170 people with gifts totaling $100,000. The second year they called 270 persons. The third year they made more than 500 calls and the result was $1 million in gifts.

Bud Cooper, CFRE
Hartsook Companies, Inc. (Kansas City, Mo.)

Donor recognition: Acknowledge every gift regardless of the amount.

Florence Cole
My Sisters' Place (Hartford, Conn.)

CHAPTER 14
THE CLOCK
IS TICKING

"NEVER PUT OFF TILL TOMORROW WHAT YOU CAN DO TODAY."

In addition to his many lasting contributions, Benjamin Franklin left us with timeless wisdom on the subject of time. His advice is particularly relevant to saying thank you to donors. Organizations should have a well-conceived plan in place to acknowledge gifts – a process that should begin the moment a gift arrives.

Thank you's tend to have a short shelf life. The sooner a donor receives an acknowledgement, the fresher the sentiment. Some groups use 48 hours as their benchmark. It would not be bad to shoot for 24. Not only will your quick turnaround reflect gratitude, but it will also demonstrate the efficiency of your office.

Set up a monetary gift acceptance policy that runs like clockwork. The instant a check, cash or credit card gift hits your office, the clock is ticking. Every development office, depending on the size of the staff and the organization, will do things a little differently. However, every office needs a fool-proof method of acknowledging each and every gift in a timely fashion.

Gifts over a certain amount might receive a note from the development director. Amounts above that might get a note or a call from a board member. The organization's president or executive director might acknowledge higher levels of giving. Periodically review your system to make sure donors are receiving the prompt thanks they deserve.

A timely word of sincere thanks is not just for major donors. Every gift, no matter the size, should be acknowledged. You never know when a donor is testing the waters. One donor took his first steps of philanthropy by sending modest amounts to a small number of organizations. He heard nothing from one group and learned later that the organization had a policy of only sending thank you's for gifts over a certain amount. Two other groups sent form letters with envelopes for a second gift.

However, the last organization stood out from the crowd, not only sending a word of sincere thanks that reminded the donor what the gift would achieve, but also adding, "Our records indicate that this is your first gift. We welcome you to a special group of individuals. Your 'new donor package' will arrive soon." This small, personal touch set the organization apart from the others. When the package arrived, it gave the donor an opportunity to send a second gift. Not surprisingly, another thank you arrived promptly. The donor was soon sending regular monthly checks, then larger checks and ultimately added the organization to his will.

The IRS may only require acknowledgments of individual gifts of $250 or more, but do you really want to use the Internal Revenue Service as your standard of demonstrating donor appreciation?

"A Stitch In Time Saves Nine."

If you send a written thank you for a major gift, be sure to mention any specific preferences or designations the donor has made. Was it for endowment or for capital? Was the gift given in cash or in-kind gifts? Make it clear that the donor was clearly heard and understood and that his wishes were followed to the letter.

Remember the rules your mother had for writing thank-you notes for Christmas and birthday presents: Give a friendly greeting, mention the gift, explain how it was or will be used, say thanks, and finish with a cordial closing. Acknowledging gifts with promptness and sincerity is "a stitch in time" and one of the most powerful means for retaining donors.

Thank-you notes are just one of the many ways to acknowledge a gift and to demonstrate appreciation. Small gifts given around the holidays are an additional gesture of thanks. Some creative organizations find ways to tie an appreciation gift to the mission. A group that helps women in ThirdWorld nations launch their own businesses, buys handmade gifts to give to donors. Donors not only receive a token of appreciation, but they get to see their financial gifts in action. Since so many children benefit from the work of Habitat for Humanity, one group established "Habitots" as a way for the children to give back to others. Ornaments and other items made by the children are sent to donors as a way of demonstrating appreciation.

For larger gifts, you may want to go beyond one "thank you." There is nothing wrong with following up a card or letter with a personal call from someone else in the organization.

If the development director sent the letter, maybe the executive director can make a call to express her personal appreciation as well.

Saying thank you is not only the right thing to do, it is a wonderful and natural way to keep the conversation going. Every time a donor makes a contribution, respond with an acknowledgement and personal word of thanks. Through those actions – either by mail, phone or in person – more opportunities will arise for sharing back and forth. The goal is to continue the dialogue in order to increase a donor's sense of connectedness with the organization. Building donor loyalty is one of the greatest functions and outcomes of showing appreciation and recognition, and greater donor loyalty means greater gifts down the road.

By the way, when it comes time to recognize donors in an annual report or other publication, make sure that a great deal of attention to detail is given to this process. Only recognize those donors who have agreed to make their gifts public. Double-check the list to ensure that no one's name is missing and confirm that the spelling and title for every name is correct. This is one more "stitch" that can save at least "nine" problem stitches later. Leave a donor's name off one of these lists and you will have a lot of mending to do in the future.

"YOU MAY DELAY, BUT TIME WILL NOT."

A donor wants to be told that her gift matters and she wants to be told while the ink on her check is still wet. Development offices are busy places. Saying thank you can appear to be a lower priority than some of the other urgent tasks – until you start losing regular donors. Believe me, saying thank you to all your donors – especially those who give significant gifts – is one of the most powerful things you can do as a fundraiser. Do it well and you will open wide the doors for future successful solicitations.

Incorporate fresh information into your notes, calls or visits. Along with an acknowledgement of the gift, offer a quick story of how the gift is being used. Provide a new statistic that highlights the work you do. Remind donors that "because of their gifts, all this is possible."

Most important, do it today – while there is still time.

BEST PRACTICES

For gifts received via e-mail, follow up beyond just an e-mail reply. Get on the phone. Call them and say thank you. It often turns into a bigger gift. It allows you to connect.

Robert Crandall, CFRE
American Baptist Churches USA (Valley Forge, Pa.)

We are a very small staff and volunteer fundraising group. I'm always afraid the 'thank you' will be overlooked or not sent in a timely manner because everyone is doing two or three jobs at the same time. So, the day the pledge arrives in the office an immediate thank-you letter goes out. If the gift/pledge is from someone I know personally, I always hand write a one- or two-line note at the bottom of the printed letter. I've had many donors comment that they appreciated the personal note. We then go straight to the database and enter 'a thank you has been sent to the donor' and the date.

Dorothy E. Kennedy
Girl Scouts Tiak Council, Inc. (McAlester, Okla.)

Send thank you's in person and in tangible ways to each donor, no matter how large or small the gift.

Joni Brown
UHV American Humanics (Victoria, Tex.)

Immediately acknowledge all gifts – no later than 48 hours.

Anthony Bir
Oblate Missions (San Antonio, Tex.)

Personally hand write thank-you notes. Call personally to thank a donor for a gift.

Tiffany Sandholm
Big Brothers and Big Sisters of Gallatin County
(Bozeman, Mont.)

Acknowledge donations within 48 hours.

Ellen Ayoub
Ayoub & Associates (Las Vegas, Nev.)

Make a personal telephone call of thanks to all donors of $25 or more.

Chris McCormick, CFRE
Wesleyan Homes (Georgetown, Tex.)

We're essentially a start-up right now with a history. So our best practice is recognizing each donor with a thank-you letter within 24 hours, and a phone call from a board member within three days.

Sherry Hogan
Jacksonville Museum of Modern Art (Jacksonville, Fla.)

Thank the donor within 24 hours of receiving the gift.

Ken Forbes
World Vision Canada (Mississauga, Ontario)

CHAPTER 15
WHO SHOULD SAY THANK YOU?

Who should have the responsibility of saying thank you to donors? The short answer is everyone. Just as organizations have begun to accept that solicitation is everyone's job (including the president or executive director, board members and those closest to the organization), so, too, is demonstrating appreciation and giving donors the recognition they deserve.

Depending on the level of giving that an organization is accustomed to, systems should be established to involve a variety of people in the process. Showing appreciation is not only important for donors, but by involving board members, volunteers and even clients in the act of saying thanks, you help create a climate of gratitude for your organization. You lessen the risk that your nonprofit will grow complacent or that anyone will take donors or their gifts for granted.

Certainly for major donors, it is important that they receive personal attention from someone they greatly admire – maybe that is the president, but perhaps a call from a certain board member would be more meaningful. Just as you learn to predict who would be the best person to conduct a particular donor solicitation, you should use good judgment in delegating donor thank you's.

BEYOND A GIFT ACKNOWLEDGEMENT

Not all gifts are created equally. Therefore, not all gifts should be given the same show of appreciation. Following the initial acknowledgment, find other ways to have people in your organization say thank you to donors.

In addition to the development director, executive director and board members, here are some other avenues for delegating expressions of appreciation and recognition.

I. Have those who are served say thanks.

Donors want to know that their gifts make a difference. Allowing clients to express their appreciation is a wonderful way to say thank you to donors in a meaningful way.

If you enlist constituents – students who have received scholarships, mothers who have received cars, families who have received medical care for a loved one, etc. – offer helpful guidelines. Give everyone some direction about topics to include in their letter of thanks. Without introducing a strict format, provide general guidance and encouragement.

II. Have your organization say thanks.

Donors may not want you to spend a lot of money on expensive gifts. However, thoughtful gestures can be every bit as effective for assuring donors that their gifts are truly appreciated. Is a donor an art collector? What about hand-delivering an elegant coffee-table book featuring one of the donor's favorite artists? Is a donor an opera buff? What about sending tickets for two to an upcoming performance? As the saying goes, "It is the thought that counts." As long as the thought moves beyond an idea and is turned into action, it really is the meaning behind the gift that causes the donor to feel valued and appreciated. If this sounds a lot like cultivation, it is. Showing appreciation is one of the best methods for cultivating and encouraging future gifts.

III. Have your newsletters and reports say thanks.

Feature donors and their gifts in your organization's various publications and reports. Annual reports can include a list of donor categories – Gold, Silver and Bronze donors – with an asterisk by any who have upgraded their gifts in the past year.

IV. Have your buildings, grounds, funds and programs say thanks.

Naming opportunities, honorary titles and memorial displays are wonderful ways to keep saying thank you to high-caliber donors. Combine your organization's needs with opportunities to recognize the generosity of donors. Are your grounds in need of landscaping? Plant a tree in honor of a major donor. Create a small garden and sitting area in honor of another. Are you installing new computer equipment? Screensavers offer a new way to say thank you. Set up a screen that commemorates the donor's gift: "Welcome to the J. B. Jones Learning Center" in gold, centered on a blue screen for all to see.

Look around and consider the many possibilities. Find new ways to say thank you. Keep saying thanks and you will multiply your need to say thanks in the future. Whatever you do, never assume that a donor is going to give a gift simply because he or she has in the past. Nonprofit organizations are never owed the gifts they are given; they earn them.

BEST PRACTICES

The vice president of development makes personal calls to donors over $100. The executive director makes personal calls to donors over $500. We invite them to tour our facility.

Janet Arena Burns, CFRE
Clovernook Center for the Blind (Cincinnati, Ohio)

Ask the ultimate beneficiary of a donation to write a simple, personal thank you to the donor. This is especially effective coming from children (schools, daycare centers, youth groups, etc.) but works just as well no matter who's doing the writing. This helps reinforce the human element and serves as a valuable cultivation step for ongoing support.

Arliss Swartzendruber
Hartsook Companies, Inc. (Denver, Colo.)

We raise money for a burn camp. The staff take pictures and assign a child to send a thank you with the picture to the donor. The donors love it. One donor was so pleased he sent 10 kids to camp for a week. (It costs $100 to send a child to camp for a day.) If an organization donated products, their thank-you note featured the kids using those products.

Unsigned

Always remember your donors!

Gail Lamb
Illinois State University (Normal, Ill.)

Because of the tremendous impact Habitat for Humanity has on children, we are always looking for ways to engage them in our work – other than on the construction site. 'Habitots,' children supporting the work of Habitat, decorate small wooden house ornaments cut out by local woodworker groups. Adult volunteers help with details such as writing our organization's name and year on the back. These one-of-a-kind ornaments have many uses: donor appreciation gifts to anyone making donations throughout the year; as part of our alternative holiday gift program; and gifts to local officials, community partners and prospective donors. Teachers who lead the children in decorating the ornaments integrate the experience into their lesson plan. I see the ornaments hanging in offices all over Macon!

Michele Neely
Macon Area Habitat for Humanity (Macon, Ga.)

Lead volunteers send handwritten thank-you cards to donors of $2,000 and above.

Kristi Shepard
United Way of Dane County (Madison, Wisc.)

Of the many forms of recognition for our largest donors, the simple gesture of a dinner at your home makes a lasting impact. It requires that you take time to establish a relationship with that donor on a more meaningful level than we have come to expect. Our largest donor said it best: 'This works!'

Sam Culotta, Jr.
YMCA of Southern Nevada (Las Vegas, Nev.)

CHAPTER 16
CREATIVE RECOGNITION AND APPRECIATION

IS YOUR DONOR RECOGNITION DUE FOR AN UPDATE?

Have you walked into a house and, just by the colors of the walls, rugs and appliances, been able to date the decor? Avocado green and Harvest gold, circa 1960. Teal and mauve, the 80s. The same goes for the cut of your hair and hem of your pants. Today's must-have can quickly become tomorrow's ho-hum.

Interestingly, the same is true of some forms of recognition. At one time, a plaque was nearly the most prestigious gift of recognition a donor could receive. Then came the growing popularity of the brick – many small naming opportunities brought together in a tangible way to convey that "I am only one person, but together we can make a difference." Donor Trees, where names are affixed to leaves and joined together in a display, remain a popular venue for recognizing gifts. Often found hanging in church and hospital lobbies, they not only showcase donor names, but they double as artwork.

As effective as these types of recognition can be, it is important for organizations to step back and consider new and personalized ways of honoring their donors. Do not simply follow the crowd. Find a way to surprise and impress your donors in order to build loyalty and secure future gifts. Particularly with the proliferation of new non-profits, donors will expect (and appreciate) something a little different.

POINT AND CLICK

Newspaper articles with accompanying photos have always been a good way to give donors public recognition for their generous gifts. Technology has made that job even easier. Always keep a digital camera on hand. Keep one at the office and make sure one is available at every fundraising event. E-mail donors with a photo and a word of thanks immediately following a fundraiser. Forward a copy to the donor's local paper with caption information.

Even if you are not personally techno-savvy, it is a good idea to find a staff person or volunteer who can take your organization to the next level of "virtual" recognition. So many opportunities have opened up for organizations to use the Internet for recognizing donors, and some of these may work well for you.

For example, naming opportunities are no longer just for buildings and equipment. Now you can take it online. What if a donor has an art collection that he intends to leave to the museum upon his death. Why not ask him to consider donating it now as a virtual exhibit? This naming opportunity will allow him to display the paintings online where they can be viewed and enjoyed by people all over the world. Even before a new wing is added to the museum ("And by the way, would you consider a gift toward the new wing as a future home for your collection?"), the donor's virtual exhibit is up and running even while the artwork is still in his possession.

One of the newest forms of techno-recognition is an interactive showcase placed in lobbies. These kiosk-type displays allow information to be changed and updated easily. The displays present the organization's story and accomplishments, and, at the same time, provide sections for donor recognition including pictures and biographies.

There are so many ways to use new technologies to show recognition. What about adding donor recognition pages to your web site? Donors can supply a biography, pictures, video clips, lifetime accomplishments, etc. Unlike plaques, donor recognition pages can be changed and updated when necessary. Once the donor page is complete, color copies can be printed and assembled in book form and given as an additional gift of recognition.

One organization honors special donors who have died. They set up a temporary memorial page on their web site to give the ultimate recognition. The page allows family members to experience the high level of respect that the organization has for the donor. After viewing the page, some families ask that gifts be given to the organization in place of sending flowers to the family.

SPECIAL DELIVERY

Even if you make use of some of the new technologies, never forget the tried and true, more traditional forms of donor recognition. Always recognize your donors in front of the people that matter most to them – friends, family, colleagues, business leaders, etc. Provide special opportunities for donors to experience behind-the-scenes events. Arrange for them to go backstage before the production, into the locker room after the game, or behind the secured storage doors of the museum. Add their names to playbills, association magazines, alumni newsletters – anything that will make them feel highly valued.

Some organizations prefer giving "consumable gifts" such as season tickets, a special dinner with notable guests, or the best seats in the house on opening night. The beauty of these perks is that you can give them again next year, and they are not only appreciated, they are anticipated. Honestly, how many certificates of appreciation can one donor receive and still feel genuinely appreciated?

Whatever means you choose to make your donors feel valuable, it is very important to establish a creative donor recognition program that reflects your organization's distinctiveness. Donor recognition may happen at the end of the process ...

- Identify prospective donors
- Research information about your donors
- Cultivate donor relationships
- Solicit gifts
- Acknowledge gifts
- Show appreciation
- Give donors the recognition they deserve...

but that certainly does not mean that it should be a last priority.

Give donors their due and watch their gratitude translate into future gifts – BIG GIFTS – for your organization.

BEST PRACTICES

The Memphis Child Advocacy Center found a creative, inexpensive way to recognize our top 100 donors each year. The week of Valentine's Day, volunteers deliver fresh-baked cookies to our most generous supporters. The cookie dough is donated and a local professional kitchen bakes them for free. Volunteers paint boxes with red, pink and purple hearts, and tie the boxes with ribbon. The donors love getting the surprise delivery. And they appreciate that the gift comes from other volunteers and donors, and isn't a pricey gift we have purchased for them.

Virginia Stallworth
Memphis Child Advocacy Center (Memphis, Tenn.)

Always have a camera at events so you can take photos of major donors (or potential donors). Send the picture to them – with a thank-you – within 24 hours.

Amanda Place, CFRE
UA Presents (Tucson, Ariz.)

For a unique donor recognition gift, ask the visual arts department at your local college or university to create a uniquely designed gift as a class project. You certainly will receive plenty of ideas and might find a sculpture, platter, tile, painting or sketch to provide that special touch for your donors.

Tami T. Druzba
Hartsook Companies, Inc. (Ft. Worth, Tex.)

As part of our capital campaign for a new women and children's shelter, we introduced the Building Hope Picket Fence Project. Donors honor or remember someone by purchasing a picket in the wooden fence that will surround the shelter. For a minimum donation of $25, the honoree's name is engraved onto the picket. This is a variation on the 'name on a brick' strategy and has proven a nice, visible and out-of-the-ordinary way for the public to gain involvement in our campaign. The pickets sold out fast.

Marcia Paulson
YWCA of Fargo-Moorhead (Fargo, N.D.)

Our stewardship reports include a written overview (from planning to clean up and most of the steps in-between), original copies of newspaper or newsletter stories and pictures, copies of ads, copies of testimonials we received and 15 to 20 photos that on their own would tell the story. Donors love this. This seems a much better way than a couple of pages of text with a cover letter. Most important, it vividly demonstrates the value and importance we placed on their gift.

Donna E. Bridges
Botanica, The Wichita Gardens (Wichita, Kan.)

We started giving away chocolate at our annual dinner. It really put a stamp on our event.

Byron S. Johnson
East Bay Local Asian Development Corporation
(Oakland, Calif.)

As a thank you to donors, we selected a resident (our organization is a residential center for mentally handicapped individuals). We did a booklet on her life at the center. It featured scenes of her and her roommate, them at the movies, etc. We sent it to donors so they could 'see' whom they were helping. We also sent a framed plaque that allowed donors to name the scholarship for one year (in the name of a loved one).

Cathi Johnson
The Baddour Center (Senatobia, Miss.)

Celebrate the philanthropy of others. Maybe your best donor, or your best prospect, is making a major gift to another organization. Send a note of acknowledgement to the donor. It illustrates that you and your organization have a big-picture understanding of your community and an 'abundance' mentality. No one ever gets ahead belittling other people's fundraising initiatives.

Robert G. Swanson
Hartsook Companies, Inc. (Wichita, Kan.)

MORE BEST
PRACTICES

BOARD DEVELOPMENT

My 34-member Board of Directors consists of the nation's most respected cable telecommunications executives. At meetings, they're ready for fierce conversations that focus on reality. So, there's always a risk of engaging them, but losing control. Three planning techniques help me manage the agenda without restraining the dialogue: (1) Carefully order topics with those that must be resolved up front. (2) Tell them the goal for each topic. (3) Minimize presentations so there's plenty of time for discussion.

Robert C. Russo
The Cable Center (Denver, Colo.)

We regularly schedule lunch with board members throughout the year. We do this as individuals, not groups.

Wayne Groner
Labette County College Foundation (Parsons, Kan.)

Retreats are a strong means to train, motivate and strengthen board members.

Gwyn Lister, CFRE
Accelerated Income Methods (Corte Madera, Calif.)

Give board members a gift basket, personalized photos, a scarf or tie.

Terri Lowery
The Orpheum Theatre/Memphis Development Foundation
(Memphis, Tenn.)

We prepare Board members to cultivate and solicit prospective Board members. Each current member spends an hour with the executive director learning about our programs and services. We also help them acquire proper terminology and key messages. Through the variety of contacts from Board and community members we construct our prospective member list, then our development committee aligns the prospects with the diversity we seek. The Board approves the list. Through personal contact, tours of our facility, meetings with the executive director, printed materials and follow-up, we have been able to secure many new Board members.

Peggy Marie Smith
Community Children's Project (Jackson Hole, Wyo.)

During nomination process for the board, bring in prospective board members for a tour of the organization before asking them to join. Give them a formal orientation and tell them how much they are expected to give annually.

Susan Corrington, CFRE, LCSW
Edgewood Children's Center (St. Louis, Mo.)

Throw conferences and retreats at great locations.

Richard Adams
Free Will Baptist (Antioch, Tenn.)

Define board roles. Evaluate committees two times a year to drive your process.

Sherry Hogan
Jacksonville Museum of Modern Art (Jacksonville, Fla.)

Recruit board members as adding specific ingredients in a successful recipe. Use organization goals and fund development plans to strategically select prospects who have specific skills and experience related to your goals and objectives.

Sherry Weber
DePaul Health Center Foundation (Bridgeton, Mo.)

Ensure your board has how-to books; continue to provide them training tips on a variety of topics. This builds your current board and mentors for new board members as they arrive.

Marci Bowling
Development Center of the Ozarks (Springfield, Mo.)

Build and maintain ongoing relationships with trustees.

Dan Douglas
The Volunteer Center (Owensboro, Ky.)

MANAGEMENT

Think like a businessperson when running your organization.

Mary Imig
Nebraska Children's and Families Foundation (Lincoln, Neb.)

To foster nonprofit collaboration and share overhead costs, our organization moved into the offices of another nonprofit. We share some functions and referrals.

John Fellerer
Habitat for Humanity of the West Valley (El Mirage, Ariz.)

Keep a beginner's mind. Never assume there is nothing anybody can teach you.

Nicole Turner
Summit R&D Group (Lenexa, Kan.)

To strengthen Board and staff achievement use business-assessment tools such as Force Field Analysis or SWOT (Strengths, Weaknesses, Opportunities, Threats). Hold a retreat with the Board and staff. Begin the evaluation with the mission. Is there a clear mission statement? Has the mission shifted over the years? Continue working through the different programs and services. This is a non-threatening way to educate the Board and increase staff performance.

Diana M. Watt, CFRE
Phi Sigma Pi National Honor Fraternity (Lancaster, Pa.)

Treat staff and donors the way you want to be treated. Always keep a posture of humility as a leader.

Jennie S. Amison
Gemeinschaft Home, Inc. (Harrisonburg, Va.)

Use games as a teaching tool.

Sue Noakes
Girl Scouts of Dogwood Trails Council, Inc. (Springfield, Mo.)

We encourage a 'word of the week' that the staff directs.

Bradley Hoopes
Water Street Rescue Mission (Lancaster, Pa.)

Endowment covers operational costs.

Josef Natale
United Way of Southeastern New England (Providence, R.I.)

Maintain individual and personal contact with board members and volunteers.

Jean Jenkins
Community Medical Center Foundation (Missoula, Mont.)

ET CETERA

We work with two companies that liquidate corporate products and/or assets. We get about 10 cents on the liquidated dollar to help feed the poor here and abroad.

Jane Kelley
Gift Angels (Johnsburg, Mo.)

We're listed in the phone book. The name "hospice" gets people to us because of its strong recognition. We're using the Yellow and White pages to give people a place to find us.

Annie Erker
Hospice Foundation of St. Louis (St. Louis, Mo.)

Take a best practice/success from the past, add variable twists, refine and reintroduce. Success builds success.

John Velde
Pearl & Associates (Peoria, Ill.)

Good customer service requires that you respond to all e-mails, phone calls and other inquiries quickly – within 24 hours at the latest. If you cannot do so, you should pass the message along to someone else who can at least make contact and recognize the initial correspondence. This holds just as true for inquiries from within your organization as those coming from the outside.

Larry Pierce
U. S. Army Corps of Engineers (Harper's Ferry, Va.)

Continually read up on current philanthropic trends.

Jon Nelson
The Salvation Army (St. Paul, Minn.)

Our organization is fairly new to traditional fundraising. We've relied on grant writing for much of our support in the past. To expand our resource base we recognized the need to create a strategic development plan. Rather than working in a void, we responded to an RFP offering planning support from a local university's graduate school of management. Through such a joint venture, their students will have opportunity to develop a strategic plan for an actual organization facing real issues, real mission, real clients and a real need. We will benefit from the collective experience of the students (many of whom have nonprofit experience) and their instructor. This is a win-win for everyone.

Andrea Joseph, CFRE
Rhode Island Children's Crusade (Roseville, Minn.)

I carry a three-ring binder with me everywhere. I write down ideas, suggestions, messages and things I need to accomplish. At the end of the day I refer back to my notes. I prioritize my tasks while giving new thought to the ideas on the pages. As a staff of one, this daily journal is a very important tool for keeping our operation moving smoothly.

Olga Nichols
Waimea Community Education (Kamuela, Hawaii)

INDEX

A

B

D

E

F

G

ABOUT THE AUTHOR

Bob Hartsook as an author, speaker and consultant, has influenced the direction of philanthropy. His thoughts and experiences have helped both the novice and the experienced fundraiser in closing significant gifts.

Speaking to thousands of professionals and volunteers, he focuses on the demands of raising funds today. His proprietary Integrated Fundraising Campaign℠ has helped countless institutions achieve maximum financial goals. On the pages of the most popular fundraising journals, magazines and newsletters, including *The Chronicle of Philanthropy, Planned Giving Today, Advancing Philanthropy, Philanthropy International, The NonProfit Times* and many others, he articulates the significant challenges facing fundraisers. Dr. Hartsook is the author of five other best-selling books: *Closing that Gift!, How to Get Million Dollar Gifts and Have Donors Thank You!, Getting your Ducks in a Row!, Nobody Wants to Give Money Away!* and *On the Money!*

Prior to starting Hartsook and Associates in 1987, now Hartsook Companies, Inc., Dr. Hartsook served as

Executive Vice President of the Kansas Engineering Society and Vice President of Colby Community College, Washburn University and Wichita State University. At Wichita State he was named president of the Board of Trustees.

Bob's many honors include receiving the 2004 Spirit of Philanthropy Award from the Center on Philanthropy at Indiana University and being recognized as a Distinguished Alumnus by Emporia State University (Emporia, Kan.).

Dr. Hartsook holds a Bachelor of Arts in Economics, a Master of Science in Counseling, a Juris Doctor and a Doctor of Education. He lives with his son Austin, on Wrightsville Beach, North Carolina.

Hartsook Companies serves more than 250 clients across the country annually and has helped more than 1,400 organizations raise billions of dollars.

Dr. Robert F. Hartsook
Chairman and CEO
Hartsook Companies, Inc.
P. O. Box 782890
Wichita, KS 67278-2890
Telephone: 316.630.9992
Facsimile: 316.630.9993
e-mail: bob@hartsookcompanies.com
web site: http://www.hartsookcompanies.com

ABOUT ASR PHILANTHROPIC PUBLISHING

ASR Philanthropic Publishing serves the fundraising and philanthropic community with a variety of publications designed to inform and educate, as well as stimulate thought and discussion by professionals throughout the United States.

ASR publications include newsletters, books and monographs, as well as audio and video products. In addition, ASR's Reference collection of monographs and books can be purchased in small or large quantities. Large-quantity orders may qualify for discounts, and customized imprinting and binding to meet your organization's reference needs.

ASR Philanthropic Publishing has an active custom-publishing division that creates books, newsletters, brochures and other print material for use by fundraising and philanthropic organizations. The firm is available to consult on your organization's specific communication needs.

To order or receive information about any of ASR's publications or programs, please contact:

ASR Philanthropic Publishing
P. O. Box 782648
Wichita, Kansas 67278
Telephone: 316.634.2100
Facsimile: 316.630.9993
e-mail: info@ASRpublishing.com
web site: www.ASRpublishing.com

ASR
REFERENCE
COLLECTION

Closing that Gift!

(1998, ASR Philanthropic Publishing), Bob Hartsook's first book, now is in its third printing, has attained critical acclaim and sales success since its initial publication. Reviewers have said: "impressive . . . an important hands-on guide . . . serious fundraisers won't just read this book, they'll use it every day." 160 pages.

A perennial best seller at the AFP International Conference, Bob Hartsook's *How to Get Million Dollar Gifts and Have Donors Thank You!* (1999, ASR Philanthropic Publishing) recounts 101 real-life stories of million-dollar gifts made by average Americans. 281 pages.

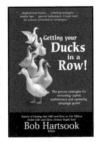

Getting your Ducks in a Row!
(2001, ASR Philanthropic Publishing) combines the in-depth knowledge of a textbook with humor, interest and enthusiasm. The book brings together more than 20 outstanding authors and sources providing a toolbox of fundraising strategies. Edited by Bob Hartsook. 240 pages.

Nobody Wants to Give Money Away!
(2002, ASR Philanthropic Publishing) is perhaps Bob Hartsook's most insightful book. Reviewers call it motivating, entertaining and right on target. Through stories from more than two decades of fundraising experience, Bob explores the nine fundraising truths essential to success. Illustrations by Mark Litzler. 127 pages.

On the Money!
(2004, ASR Philanthropic Publishing) is an enlightening collection of success stories from nonprofit fund-raising campaigns nationwide. Written by Bob Hartsook. It illuminates 25 successful funding campaigns by dynamic and effective organizations, along with Consultants' Tips – lessons learned from those who managed the project, and easily applied to any nonprofit. 207 pages.

For more information or to order these books,
check out the ASR web site:
WWW.ASRPUBLISHING.COM

BUSINESS REPLY MAIL
FIRST-CLASS MAIL   PERMIT NO. 5112   WICHITA KS

POSTAGE WILL BE PAID BY ADDRESSEE

ASR PHILANTHROPIC PUBLISHING
PO BOX 782648
WICHITA 67278-9680

BUSINESS REPLY MAIL
FIRST-CLASS MAIL   PERMIT NO. 5112   WICHITA KS

POSTAGE WILL BE PAID BY ADDRESSEE

HARTSOOK COMPANIES INC
PO BOX 782890
WICHITA KS 67278-9670